Adeline Shimmelmann, W. S. Foggitt, Otto Funcke

Adeline Countess Schimmelmann

Glimpses of my Life at the German Court, among Baltic Fishermen and Berlin

Socialists

Adeline Shimmelmann, W. S. Foggitt, Otto Funcke

Adeline Countess Schimmelmann
Glimpses of my Life at the German Court, among Baltic Fishermen and Berlin Socialists

ISBN/EAN: 9783337127558

Printed in Europe, USA, Canada, Australia, Japan

Cover: Foto ©Andreas Hilbeck / pixelio.de

More available books at **www.hansebooks.com**

ADELINE
COUNTESS SCHIMMELMANN

ADELINE
COUNTESS SCHIMMELMANN

GLIMPSES OF MY LIFE AT THE GERMAN
COURT, AMONG BALTIC FISHERMEN AND
BERLIN SOCIALISTS AND IN PRISON

INCLUDING

'A HOME ABROAD,' BY PASTOR OTTO FUNCKE

EDITED BY

W. SMITH FOGGITT

PASTOR OF THE ENGLISH REFORMED
CHURCH, HAMBURG

WITH PORTRAITS AND ILLUSTRATIONS

Third Thousand

LONDON
HODDER AND STOUGHTON
27 PATERNOSTER ROW
1896

Edinburgh: T. and A. CONSTABLE, Printers to Her Majesty

EDITOR'S PREFACE

Countess Adeline Schimmelmann, whose name is a household word in Germany and Scandinavia, is already well known to many English Christians as a lady of high social position whose devotion to Jesus Christ has placed her in the front rank of the noble band who in recent times have 'suffered the loss of all things,' and taken 'joyfully the spoiling of their goods,' for His sake, and who have 'gone forth without the camp, bearing His reproach.' Only narrowly has she missed the crown of martyrdom.

Portions of the following narrative are already familiar to German and Danish readers. 'A Home Abroad,' by Otto Funcke, in which the famous Bremen Pastor describes his visit to some of the scenes associated with the Baltic Mission, appeared a few years ago in a volume edited by his equally famous friend, Emil Frommel of Berlin. A translation of Funcke's testimony has been issued in Denmark, together with notes of other aspects of her Mission, written by the Countess herself.

These, however, contain only the record of her offence against conventional custom, in forsaking the brilliant circles of fashion for obscure toil among neglected fishermen, and in attempting the task, so often deemed impracticable, of living in literal obedience to the precepts of Christ.

'If,' said one who heard the Countess, 'we were to do as *she* tells us, Society would be revolutionised!' 'Even so,' was the answer; 'but if it be admitted that Society is not ideally perfect, and if the change contemplated is to be the free and spontaneous creation of the spirit of Christian love, and of joyful loyalty to the truth enshrined in the teaching of Jesus, this revolution of peace will be by no means a calamity.'

To this position Countess Schimmelmann attained only by dint of painful, and, for the most part, of unaided, effort. Now, for the first time, in response to many appeals, she is supplementing the earlier narrative with a recital of some of the influences and tendencies which issued in her present mode of life, and with a brief account of the terrible persecution to which, on account of her work, she was subjected.

The Countess is no visionary theorist. With a

keen intellect, warm sympathies, and unfailing good nature, she has identified herself with the cause of the poor, the neglected, and the suffering, and never fails to evoke reciprocal confidence. At present she is making a close study of the social question on English soil. Whenever opportunity arises she converses with working men and women, and is delighted at the kindliness with which they respond to her inquiries and accept her counsels. Speaking quite recently in a third-class compartment of a London underground railway-train to a group of workmen, who on entering had somewhat roughly jostled and hurried her and her companion, the Countess quickly won their interest and good-will. To the older men she addressed careful questions, and proffered good advice to a stalwart young Socialist of nineteen. Presently a ragged little man in one corner of the compartment said—

'You ain't English, ma'am?'

'No, I am not.'

'Are you French?'

'No, I am German—or Danish.'

'And I,' said he, looking as if he felt that there was

somewhere a bond of sympathy between them—'I was born in Holland.'

'Oh, then you understand Low German?'

'Yes!'—and to the astonishment of the company a few sentences were exchanged in that pleasing but mysterious dialect.

This stirring up of old memories quite overcame the Dutchman, and without giving a moment's warning as to his intention, he had drawn two large oranges from the recesses of his rags and placed them quickly but respectfully on the Countess's lap.

'Thank you,' she said, touched by the unexpected gift; 'these will please my boys,'—and reaching past the young Socialist that she might shake hands with the giver, she asked, 'And what do *you* do?'

'I sell *them*,' he said, pointing with a beaming face to the oranges.

The workmen left the carriage looking as if they had received more than they had deserved, and were thankful.

W. S. F.

HAMBURG, *January* 1896.

CONTENTS

INTRODUCTION

As there are many experiences I have passed through which, if fully related, might involve persons still living, and others connected with my life at Court and the political events and personages of my time, which I would rather did not appear until after my death, I will only for the present endeavour to gratify the expressed wish of many friends by the following narrative. Although somewhat loosely linked together, it may yet present a fairly complete picture of the events of my life.

A. S.

YACHT 'DUEN,' ROTHERHITHE,
    LONDON, *January* 1896.

CHILDHOOD AND AT COURT

A

I WAS born in the Castle of Ahrensburg in Holstein on the 19th July 1854.

My father was the late Danish Count of the County of Lindenborg—'Lehnsgreve Schimmel-mann of Lindenborg in Denmark.' As I was the fourth daughter born to my parents, and had been preceded by only one brother, my advent was somewhat disappointing to my mother. I was a quiet and healthy child, however, and my mother's disappointment was modified by my good looks and peaceable disposition. The muscular tenacity of infants is well known, and received a striking illustration from my conduct when I had attained the tender age of five weeks. To test my infantile strength my parents allowed me to take hold of a light chair, and, on my being drawn away, I am said to have lifted the chair from the ground.

The experiment was an awkward one, and left a mark on my arm for life. Thus early did I begin to evince a strong character, and to show great unwillingness to let slip anything I took in hand!

The Castles of my father were built and maintained in the grand style which is only to be found on the estates of great families in England and Denmark. In none of the many Courts which I have since visited have I found the manner of life appreciably different from that to which I was accustomed in my ancestral homes.

My dear father was not fond of display. His personal tastes were simple and moderate, and were in marked contrast with my mother's love of magnificence and luxury, which was restrained and balanced by his severe simplicity.

When I was three years of age I was taken into society for the first time. This was on the occasion of a dinner-party at the Court of the beautiful Queen Caroline Amalie at Fredensborg, and I am sorry to confess that the experiment—a premature one, perhaps—was not a success.

I failed to prove my fitness for the Court by refusing to kiss the Queen's hand, frankly telling her that I would much prefer to kiss her cheek! The Queen, however, was very fond of children, and was greatly amused at my misconduct. She took me on her lap, and petted me, and insisted that I should remain with her the whole day. I very well remember how charmed I was at lunch at being allowed to help myself and to select the sandwiches I liked best, instead of being fed by my nurse with bread and milk as I had been wont.

Looking back I can still see the kind eyes of the Queen upon me, and I remember with pleasure the stock-rose which she broke for me in her garden. How well it had been for me if my recollection could not pass beyond that pretty scene! But alas! as the day went on I fell into deep disgrace. Despite my poor mother's protestations, Her Majesty insisted on installing me at her dinner-table between two young gentlemen. At first the arrangement succeeded admirably, but when I saw my mother, who sat beside the Queen at the other end of the table, making signs to my neighbours that they were not to allow me to partake of a splendid red dish which had been brought to us (it was lobster, I fear), I raised my voice in a prolonged wail of opposition! Instantly my mother sent one of the footmen to take me out, but, declaring that I could go by myself, I slipped down from my chair, ran up to the Queen, and, clinging with both hands to a fold of her wide black satin dress, I entreated her not to send me out until I had got some of 'that there,' pointing to a dish of beautiful peaches in front of her. She placed one on a plate, and I retired, as gracefully as I could, to an adjoining room, the footman following me with the booty. I have a vague fear that in my place of retreat I had the misfortune to break a doll belonging to the Princess Dagmar (the Dowager-Empress of Russia). Here my memory happily fails me.

Several years passed before another appearance at Court was deemed desirable. At home I was sometimes brought in to dessert in my white muslin dress and red shoes, and I can recall occasions on which I was placed on the large dining-table, and allowed to move about among the old Meissen porcelains and silver vases, until I finally seated myself in the midst of a large basket of flowers *vis-à-vis* with my father, who would then give me my share of the sweets.

I cannot recall all my governesses and nurses, but I remember that they were French, and German, and English. My first nurse, 'Chatinka,' I distinctly remember, and *the vivid impression remains with me that she was a pious Christian.* At that early age I spoke several languages, and thus began the cultivation of a linguistic facility which was afterwards to be of great service to me at Court, and, later on, in my work among the sailors and workmen of different nationalities. My French, in the days in which I used to be placed 'on the table,' was, I am told, greatly appreciated by my father's guests.

We were eleven children in all. The sister next to me was four years older than myself, and those who came after me were boys. I therefore stood somewhat apart in the midst of my brothers and sisters, and felt the need of companionship with children of my own age and sympathies. This may in part explain a remark which my mother let fall when I was in my sixth year: 'She is not at all like my own child,' she said, 'she is so entirely different from all the others.' The flight of years seemed only to widen the gulf of separation, and the difference of inward tendency was greater, perhaps, than that of outward accident.

Now came the years of education and the stress and strain of training. Not that the process was a severe one. Nature did more for me that all my masters. It was arranged that I should do my lessons along with my brothers who were my juniors, and I was consequently under no necessity to take pains with my work, but rather regarded it in the light of a pastime. I amused myself by putting the dates and events of my history into rhyme. I greatly dislike anything mechanical, and the master whom I esteemed most highly was one who indulged me in the whim of doing my sums seated at the top of an old fir-tree in the park, and only

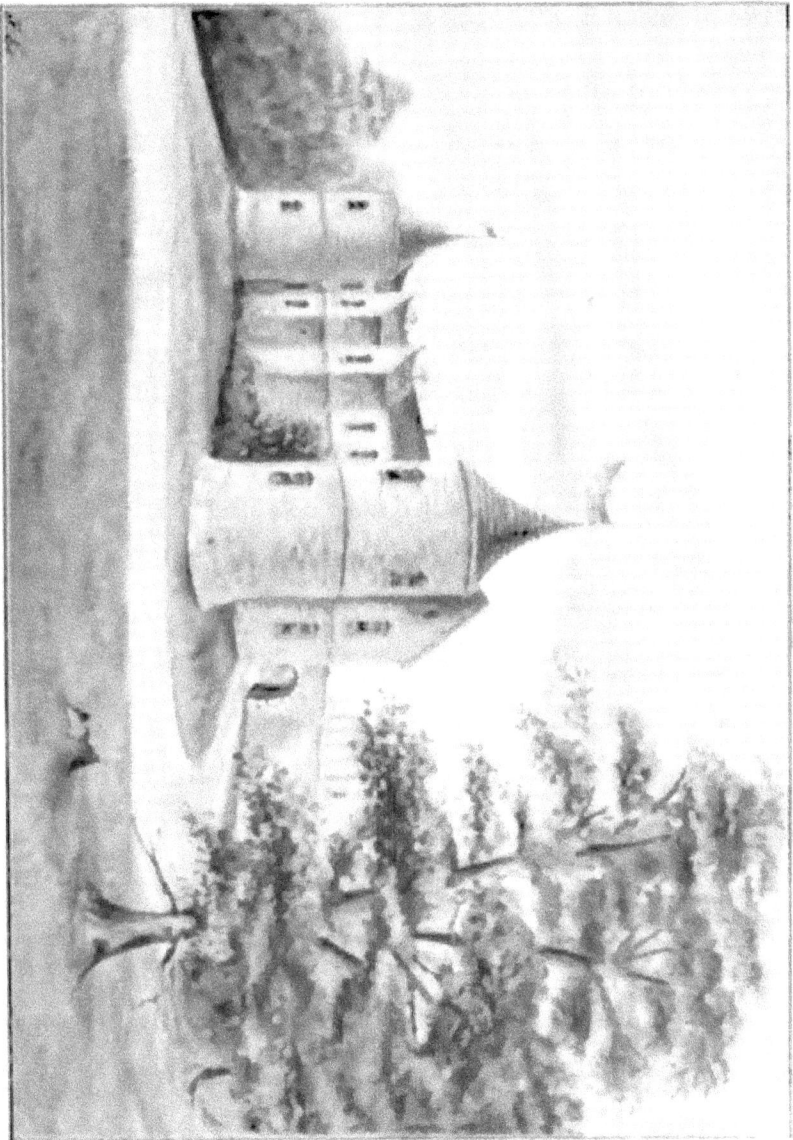

CASTLE OF THE COUNTY OF LINDENBORG, DENMARK

coming into school with the solutions. I had a wonderful gift of seeming to look exceedingly attentive, while my thoughts were wandering through the universe.

My religious training, such as it was, gave me the greatest pleasure. With the help of an old Catechism in the hands of a nursery-maid, I had learned to read before I was six years of age, and I well remember the astonishment of my governess when, on beginning to teach me its doctrinal definitions and scripture texts, she found that I could repeat from memory the whole of the first part of the Catechism. My most delightful treasure and plaything, however, was the great Picture-Bible of Schnorr of Carolsfeld. I could lie on the floor for hours together spreading its glorious pictures around me, and just living in the scenes they depicted. The fine lines of Schnorr's figures impressed themselves realistically on my young mind, and there can be little doubt that it was by them that my deep love of art, and any gift of artistic representation which I afterwards developed, were called into exercise. Their religious value

who can estimate? Catechism and picture were
alike necessary, teaching mind and heart, thought
and imagination.

At the age of seven I fell ill of fever, which
reduced me to a state of extreme weakness. I
was for a long period unable to do anything, and
I well remember with what painful frequency I
was told, 'You must not do this,' and 'You
must not do that,' and 'You will get worse if
you do not keep quiet!' I was neither expected
nor allowed to engage in the pursuits of the
other children. To a nature so fond of freedom
and so impatient of unnatural restraint these
injunctions were galling in the extreme. The
recollection of them is one of the saddest
connected with my early life.

I soon outgrew my weakness, and, with no
playfellows but my brothers, I quickly became
the wildest boy among them. Every opportunity
of taking exercise in the open air was welcome
to me. To ride in the swing, to climb the trees,
to bathe, to fish, to row—these were my greatest
pleasures. I roamed for hours in the parks, and
paid frequent visits to the fruit-trees in the

orchards. For riding on horseback I did not so much care, as we were not allowed to do this unless we were accompanied by a groom and the master of the stables, and I thought it rather irksome to be thus attended. Thus passed the happy years of youth. To them, and to the reasonable discipline and healthful recreations with which they were filled, I attribute the strength of body, clearness of mind, and over-flowing spirits which, in the Divine mercy, I have since in so rich a measure enjoyed.

The death of my mother's father, while I was yet a child, brought reflections more serious than might be thought possible in the case of one so young. An undying impression was left on my memory when, for the first time in my life, I gazed on death, and saw my aunts, who were perpetually quarrelling, unable to live at peace within sight of the still, white face. It must have been about the same time that I received my first wonderful answer to prayer. A terrible murder had been committed in Holstein by a farmer of the name of Tim Tode. In the most barbarous manner he had put to death his entire family of seven persons. Twenty stabs were found in the body of his mother. No quarrel had preceded the tragedy, and no motive could be discovered for the crime, except that he was desirous of getting possession of the farm. It was the first time I had heard of a deed so terrible, and yet it pierced me to the heart when I heard that the man was to be executed. My indignation turned to pity. Was this soul to be eternally lost? He denied his guilt, and remained obdurate in his impenitence almost to the last. With all my heart I began to pray for his salvation. When, four weeks after this, the execution took place, the papers announced that, to the astonishment of all, the murderer had confessed his guilt, and that in deep penitence for his sin he had come to the Cross of Christ and found pardon through faith in His blood. My heart was filled with joy when I heard the news, and I knew it was in answer to my prayers, although fourteen years passed away before I ventured to mention it.

This leads me to say that as a rule Christian subjects were never discussed in our home, except with the clergyman when he happened to be present. To do so was regarded as highly improper, and, indeed, hypocritical. Only when alone with my father did I sometimes venture to speak of religion. And yet the family professed to be Christian. 'Grace' was said at dinner, and there were even occasions when the Bible was read to the servants in the morning; but, as if by mutual consent, religious topics were carefully avoided during the day. This systematic suppression of religion is, I regret to say, a common thing in many distinguished families. A change is taking place in Germany in this respect, since it is supposed that the young Empress seems inclined to patronise Christianity. Hence, to a certain extent, it is allowed, and even regarded as respectable. But if you are anxious not to shock society, and do not wish to be called either a zealot or a bigot, be very careful to keep as near to the surface as you can!

One last glimpse at the fleeting years of my youth and I will pass to the equally fleeting life of the Court. At the age of fifteen I was confirmed. The ceremony took place in the chapel of the Castle, which was crowded to excess on the occasion. With the exception of one little friend, I was the only candidate, and for the space of about half an hour I was examined in the hearing of all. At that time I knew very little about experimental religion and of salvation through Christ, yet I was deeply serious and very earnest in my desire to give myself to God. The great dinner-party which followed, the guests, with all the paraphernalia of presents and congratulations, flowers and toasts, greatly disturbed me. But one event left an unfading impression on my mind. My father rose and said he would not 'drink my health.' Instead of that he would give me a word which he wished me to bear in mind through life, and to remember in eternity—it would in the present life and in the hereafter ensure my happiness: 'Seek first the Kingdom of God and His righteousness, and all these things shall be added to you.' This word have I ever kept in my heart. I am my father's child, and, as the sequel will show, it was through his influence and example, and by means of his last sufferings and death, that I was led to place 'these things' last, and to become consciously and fully the child of God by faith in Jesus Christ.

AT COURT WITH THE EMPRESS AUGUSTA

After my confirmation, I began to take an active part in the very gay life which obtained at my father's residences. Then came the Franco-Prussian War, which brought great changes. My father had never been in the army, seeing that he was a peer of Denmark; but when war was declared he offered himself as a Knight of the Order of St. John to accompany the army and attend to the wounded soldiers. His offer was the outcome of a noble nature, as he was at that time advanced in years. Many of the Berlin nobility did not share these higher motives, and became Knights of the Order of St. John as a means of bringing themselves to the notice of the Court, and of pushing their way to favour. Such a spectacle filled my young enthusiastic soul with disgust. My father was so displeased with them that he went to a little place near Metz, where he attended to the typhoid patients until he fell a

victim to the disease, and was brought home in
an extremely dangerous condition.   In the meantime one of ᴜᴉy brothers and several other relatives had enrolled themselves in the army, and
were at the seat of war.   In Germany everybody
was in a state of ecstasy.   I shared the feeling,
and it was under such emotions and conditions
as these that the rest of my childhood passed
away.

Amid the excitement of this time of war I was
led to neglect to a large extent my religious life.
It was re-awakened for a time by the death of
a sweet and pious younger brother; but my
thoughts were soon again occupied by the events
of those stirring days.   I helped to nurse the
wounded soldiers in their barracks, and when the
army returned in triumph to Berlin, I was there
to join in the enthusiastic welcome with which
the nation received them back.

It was on this occasion that I was first introduced to high life; but my mother, who had three
elder daughters to bring out, and who thought
me at that time too young to make my *début*,
determined to send me to a private school at

Dresden, where I should be under the care of an old friend of hers, a Countess Fitzthum. As I was the first daughter of my family—and the only one—to be sent from home to school, and as for several years I had enjoyed all the privileges of a grown-up young lady, I felt deeply offended at such treatment. I did not know at that time that it was—as my mother told me later—to prevent an unsuitable proposal of marriage that I was being sent away.

I loved the Countess Fitzthum, and under her influence the Christian life was again brought before me, although I did not like the forbidding aspect under which it presented itself in her school.

On leaving school I was presented at the Court of Berlin. From the first the Empress Augusta seemed to have resolved to attach me closely to her Court. My father positively declined to allow this, but it was nevertheless brought about. While he was away at one of his estates in Denmark or Sweden my mother brought me at the age of eighteen to Berlin. At first I went as a visitor, but afterwards, when my sister, who for three years at intervals had been with the Empress as lady-in-waiting, went home, I remained in her place. My father protested against my being bound by obligatory ties to the Court, and I received in consequence the highest rank of a Maid-of-honour, and was allowed to go and come as I chose.

For eighteen years of my life I was in this way attached to the Court, and I grew to love the Empress as a mother. She interested herself in my education in the most motherly way, and I have to thank her influence in a very high degree for the life which I am now leading.

The Empress was one of the noblest-minded women I have ever known, and I have been greatly grieved by the many false estimates of her character which have been circulated by people who saw her, but who certainly did not know her. Although I am reserving the recollections of my Court life for a later volume, I cannot refrain from briefly delineating the character of the Empress whom I so dearly loved, and whom I regarded rather as a mother than as an Empress. She was of an energetic disposition, and had an ardent temperament and an un-usually clear and penetrating intelligence. Her great foresight sometimes led her to act in a manner that startled many, but invariably I was able to see that her great ability and prescience were justified by the result, and that she had only acted in accordance with the necessities of the case.

The Empress was possessed of moral courage, and did not shrink from telling people the truth, although always under cover of the most perfect form. When she was convinced that a thing was right she would carry it out with great energy and ability, and at any cost. I can recall instances in which, when she saw that any one was doing wrong, and no one else had the cour-age to speak, she would arrange a private inter-view as if by accident, and during an apparently casual conversation would so convince the offender of his wrongdoing, and that in a manner so gracious, as completely to break him down. On one occasion she asked an individual who had been guilty of falsehood to accompany her in her morning walk, and spoke to him so plainly and earnestly about the sin of lying, that he must have felt the reproof of his offence more keenly than the honour of the walk. On another occasion I remember her speaking to an unruly young fellow in her private hospital in so motherly a way, laying her hand on his shoulder, that he began to weep, and promised amendment.

Her pure and noble soul hated laxity of morals and the slippery tone of conversation associated with it, and very few are able to realise the extent of her influence in this direction on the German Court so long as she was able to exercise it. I was a mere child when I came to her, and she shielded me most jealously from anything that might contaminate me. I was not allowed to read a book or attend the theatre without her consent, and I was strictly forbidden to speak to, or to return the visit of, several ladies known for their frivolity. By chance I was once standing beside one of these ladies, when the Empress turned round and said in the hearing of all present: 'My child, do not speak a word to this lady. I cannot bear the responsibility of knowing that your innocent mind is being corrupted by light talk.' She had trained me in the conviction that flirting was the greatest sin in which a woman could indulge, and I was indignant when I saw it going on. It was my custom to tell the Empress everything that happened, just as had been my wont with my mother, so that no one dared to speak foolishly or frivolously when I was near. This was why the Empress, speaking to a lady of me, said: 'Although she is but a young girl, I desire her presence at the Court festivities, because I know that no one will venture to be frivolous in her presence.'

Emancipated women were a horror to her refined, womanly nature, and not seldom did she send one of her ladies-in-waiting to bid a lady wear her dress less *decolleté*, or to leave off wearing a hat or a dress that looked too showy, or to speak or laugh less loudly. Like a true woman she did not neglect or despise taste in dress, or even elegance, when it was not vulgar. Her strong character was balanced throughout by the most exquisitely refined feminine taste. She was a queenly woman, not merely because she was an Empress, but in character. She combined the qualities of the ruling queen and the sensitive and delicate lady in the happiest way, and in a high degree. Her sincere religious belief enabled her to develop her character along the lines especially of patience and self-control. With a temper naturally fiery, she drilled herself to the practice of a saintlike self-restraint.

The Empress Augusta had on the whole so *grand* a character that commonplace people were unable to understand her. The lighter elements of society complained that her rule was too strict. She only kept their 'liberty' from becoming 'licence,' and it was only when she was laid aside by sickness, and was no longer able to act as the mistress of morals in her Court, that these people became reconciled to her rule. They then said the Empress had grown milder and more gracious. As a matter of fact, however, she had never lacked mildness. She had only used her influence to the utmost to keep the atmosphere of the Court pure and healthy. Confined by affliction to her apartments during her later years, she was unable to take cognisance of everything that occurred in high life. She was dependent on those around her, who told her only what they deemed convenient. The result was that she sometimes showed favour to people whom in the earlier days she would have passed by. That she was often greatly misunderstood need cause no surprise — she was so far above the average! Moreover, she had the habits of thought, and lived the old dignified life, of a bygone generation, with its love of form and ceremony. These had become a second nature to her; so that, although they may have seemed to some to be artificial, they were by no means unnatural to her.

The Empress was well versed in science and art, and I shall ever cherish with delight the recollection of conversations which she held with learned men of different nations, and in which she always took the lead. Such intellectual intercourse was a refreshment to her, as these distinguished men were more on a level with her strong intellectual sympathies and great mental gifts than were most of the ladies who surrounded her.

At an earlier stage of her religious life she fell into the common error of working *at* her own salvation, instead of trusting in Christ alone for salvation—of seeking to effect by works of righteousness that which can only be the gift of the Divine grace; and I can testify to the untiring zeal with which she attempted this impossible task. This tendency gave rise to the idea that she was a Roman Catholic. But I am happy to say that I know assuredly she was not.

The day before she fell into her last illness I was alone with her, and had a long and deeply interesting conversation with her respecting the central verity of our Evangelical faith—Redemption through the blood of Christ alone, without works. I had already fully surrendered myself to Christ, and the deepest longing of my heart was to be made sure of the state of my beloved Empress, from whom I had a presentiment I was soon to be separated by death. I thank God for that hour! I found her trusting by simple faith in Christ alone, and joyful in the immediate prospect of going to her heavenly home. She rejoiced when she heard how God was using me, and encouraged me to go on in the work which had been committed to my hands. Her face shone with peace and joy when she spoke of heaven, and of many dear to her and to myself who had gone before. She sent greetings to several royal personages, and asked me for the first time whether they loved Christ. Then she bade me remain for several days in Berlin, but made me promise that I would not pray that she might be spared until I came again in the spring, when she hoped to be at 'home.' Next day she became seriously ill. I could not pray that she might live, but I watched her as she peacefully passed away, and knew that she was indeed going ' Home.'

I cannot close this brief sketch of the Empress Augusta without adding a word that may throw light on many of her acts which led to her being misunderstood. Speaking to me once of men in general, and of the masculine character, she said : ' Because they are strong they are apt to be some- what harsh, and I think it is the woman's part to soften their harshness and to neutralise their severity. Wherever I see men at work I feel constrained to supplement their action by modifying the effects of their policy.' On this principle she acted, and yet that which she intended to be a gracious and softening influence was regarded as undue interference with the duties and rights of men, or as wilful opposition to their views and aims in the sphere of politics or society.

Of the Empress's public life and philanthropic work I cannot at present speak, nor can I dwell upon other aspects of my life during those eventful years. I had lived during that extended period as the spoiled child of the Court; so much so, that on one occasion the Crown Prince (afterwards the Emperor) Frederick introduced me to a stranger as the most highly favoured young lady of Germany, and, he added (doubtless alluding to Denmark), 'of several other kingdoms besides.'

These worldly honours had never satisfied me, and the longing for something higher and better became increasingly stronger. The gospel of Christ had been to me a beautiful poem which I had learned, and the truth of which I had always acknowledged, but never as yet had I made personal experience of the living Christ and the power of His Cross. The last year of my father's life, during which he had dangerous illnesses, revealed to me that I did not love God supremely, and my prayers at that time always culminated in the cry : 'O God, give me but a drop of the love of Christ and a spark of the fire of the Holy Spirit!' Probably my prayer had been answered, and the change was taking place before I was fully conscious of it, as I was not in communication with any one who spoke to me clearly of the truths relating to the personal and conscious realisation of salvation, be it called conversion, the new birth, or by any other name.

I was astonished to find that my views and interests did not any longer accord with those which had formerly actuated me, but the more I longed to love Christ, the more I found that I did not keep the command to love God with all my 'heart and soul and mind and strength.'

This I felt was the one essential thing, and the absence of this seemed to constitute the greatest sin. It was a short time after my father's death that God, in response to my prayer that I might love Jesus and Jesus only, had

taken all my idols away, and that I heard the
Saviour say to me: 'My child, thy salvation does
not depend upon thy love to Me, but upon My
love to thee, just as thou art.' Then broke in
upon my heart a sun of joy, in the beams of
which I still rejoice, and whose light will shine
upon me eternally.

Now my cold heart began to burn, not on
account of my love to Christ, but because of His
love to me. Now I was His, and His alone.
I felt that I must live entirely for Him. But
how to do this? I took my Bible and found
to my astonishment that there were lines laid
down clearly enough, but entirely different from
that which I had been taught to look upon as
the Christian life. For instance, how did we
keep that command of Christ: 'When thou
makest a supper, call not thy friends nor thy rich
neighbours, but call the poor and the maimed
and the halt and the blind.' But where were
the wretched to be found? Not in the royal
palace, or on the estates of my father. Then it
was that Pastor Otto Funcke, so well known in
England as the author of *Self-will and God's*

Will,[1] and other of his many works, came to my aid, and from him I received information of mission work in which ladies could engage.

For the first time in my life I understood in listening to him that I could not better show my love to Christ than by endeavouring to bring others to Him, and to do good to those for whom He died. During the meeting in the Architektenhaus, which Pastor Funcke describes in the pages which follow, I promised my Saviour that if by a lifetime of toil I could be made the means of the salvation of one soul, I would gladly live for this object.

[1] *Self-Will and God's Will.* By Otto Funcke. Translated by Elizabeth Stirling. Preface by Rev. Alex. Whyte, D.D. London : Hodder and Stoughton.

A HOME ABROAD

BY PASTOR OTTO FUNCKE

I

ON BOARD THE STEAMER 'RÜGEN'

IT was on a beautiful summer's day at noon, on the 7th August 1890, that I went on board the steamer *Rügen* in the port of Sassnitz. I was on my way to Göhren. If the reader asks, 'Where is Göhren?' my poetical friend R. would probably answer: 'On the Isle of the Blessed,' by which name he calls the Island of Rügen. Although it is not yet the 'Isle of the Blessed,' Rügen is nevertheless a most lovely island, particularly its eastern coast, which is called Jasmund. Here the shore falls off precipitously and boldly into the blue sea, which shines, especially in the morning and evening, with such exquisite colours, that even in the famous waters of Naples and Genoa nothing more beautiful is to be seen.

C

Out of the blue waves the snow-white chalk cliffs rise up perpendicularly, at some points in the wildest and most fantastic forms; for small but mighty rivulets, rising in the heart of the island, have forced their way to the ocean by breaking through the gigantic rocks, thus forming mighty ravines rivalling each other in romantic beauty. High on the tops of the white cliffs, and in the ravines leading to the sea-coast, there are the most beautiful beech-forests that can be found in Germany. Must it not be beautiful there? Yes, nothing surpasses Rügen.

While I was yet a student, my Pomeranian friends used to speak with enthusiasm of Rügen, and I was thus led to form the desire some day to visit the place. They sang a song which aptly characterises our isle, of which I can recall only the following words:—

'Weisse Möven fliegen
In der blauen Höh',
Weisse Segel wiegen
Sich auf blauer See.
Blaue Wälder krönen
Weisser Dünen Sand.
Vaterland, mein Sehnen
Ist dir zugewandt.'

Thus they sang, and my heart, so fond of travelling, awoke. Even at that time I was extremely wishful to travel to the North, but much was wanting, especially of that which is somewhat foolishly called 'the needful,' although to the traveller it is indispensable. Thirty years later God gave me the pleasure, in company with my beloved wife, of taking that journey for the first time. And we liked the beautiful island and its kind, simple inhabitants so much, that we resolved to go there for the holidays of 1890 with kith and kin—and so we did.

Although we were in ourselves a goodly company (my children alone numbered seven), yet many others joined us—amiable, good people, musical, and fond of singing, such as are rarely to be found. I will speak on another occasion of the serenades, on which occasions we went by water to our lovely Empress, who at that time was on a visit to Sassnitz with her five Princes. This, however, has nothing to do with my present journey, for on the 7th of August I was alone, and was willing to be alone.

When we were all on board, the *Rügen* went

on to Göhren. This lovely watering-place is situated on Mönchgut, a narrow peninsula extending eastwards far into the sea, and partially covered with forests. It is therefore as easy to land on the north side as on the south. To-day we chose the south side, as it was impossible, on account of the breakers, to effect a landing on the north. We therefore steamed in a wide curve round the point of the peninsula. Approaching the shore of the island we had a wonderful view. The whole Mönchgut, with its strange dunes and picturesque cottages, lay extended before our eyes in the sunshine. A fleet of at least ninety fishing-boats, great and small, lay in the anchorage. The great nets hung down like black flags from the tops of the masts to the decks, in order to be dried. The fishermen sat on deck talking and mending their nets, smoking, cooking, or lying on their backs asleep. They had recently returned from a large haul of herrings. On landing I asked the mate of the boat that took us ashore where the Countess Schimmelmann's Home for Sailors was situated. The face of the sailor, generally rather cold, brightened up on hearing the name of that lady. 'She lives there on the dune,' he replied; 'and see! she expects a visitor, for she is saluting with the flag.' I was very glad to be myself the expected one, and to see that my telegram had arrived in time, and that the lady was at home. My companion continued: 'A quarter of an hour ago the Countess herself was on the sands, and told us that this evening a strange clergy-man was to give us a Bible-lesson, and that we must all come to it.' Then I saw with pain that I should be obliged to disappoint them, as I had arranged to return the same evening to Sassnitz.

After leaving the boat I went eastward, and soon climbed the steep and very desolate sand-hill where we had seen the flag; and there, under the flag—from which point there is a magnificent view of Monchsgut, and, beyond that, of the peninsulas of Zicker and Thiessow, but particu-larly of the sea and the large fishing-fleet near the shore,—the Countess awaited me, a tall, noble figure, a maiden lady of about thirty-five years of age. She wore a white dress, and a

large but very simple straw hat.   Our greeting
was a very cordial one, for we were already
acquainted, and were sure to sail in the same
boat to the same haven.   But here I must go
back to an earlier period, as I have reached the
real object of my story.

II

FROM THE IMPERIAL PALACE TO THE LONELY SANDHILL

In February 1886 I delivered a speech in the Architektenhaus in Berlin, on the occasion of a so-called tea-evening. My speech was very mediocre, formless, and imprudent. At any rate it aroused great indignation on account of certain vague expressions which it contained, and which had been misunderstood by those who heard them. It is a great mercy that our God is able to change straw and chaff into gold. This He did on the present occasion. My intention was to show that, and in what manner, every loving Christian is called in his sphere to work for the Lord, as a fisher of men and a winner of souls. I criticised with especial severity the indifference of many ladies of the upper classes. Many of these were present, and

it has always been my principle to adapt my
remarks to those who are in my audience.
Immediately in front of me sat that evening a
very distinguished lady of about thirty years of
age, whose appearance arrested my attention.
I saw her face darkening and brightening. At
the close of my address she came forward and
told me she was the Countess Schimmelmann,
Court-lady to the Empress Augusta, who has
since died. With great emotion she told me
she had come to the Court as a mere child
of less than eighteen years of age, but that,
being a maid-of-honour, she was not bound
to the Court, but was able to come and go at
pleasure. Her father had estates in Denmark
and Holstein, and did not wish her to attach
herself to the Court. She had now been thirteen
years in Berlin, but all the splendour and luxury
that surrounded her could not relieve the great
emptiness and heaviness of her heart. Especially
on this evening had she seen how insignificant
and purposeless was her life, and that she ought
to be energetically doing something to help her
fellow-creatures.

Naturally I was gratified that my outspoken and simple words had produced such a good effect, although I did not believe it would last long. I frankly confess that I took the enthusiasm of the Countess for a Bengal light, which in the atmosphere of the Court would soon go out and leave nothing behind it. In general, if one is so easily excited, the enthusiasm is not lasting. I did not care for Court ladies at all. This is foolish, as I now know by experience. But by nature and training I distrust everything high and brilliant in this world ; and if I am honest I must affirm that the Bible does nothing to remove this distrust.

But to return to the Architektenhaus. Scarcely had I answered a few suitable or unsuitable words, when my friend Emil Frommel, whom all my readers doubtless know and like, came to fetch me. I whispered in his ear that I was in conversation with the Countess. But he took my arm and said : 'My poor fellow, be it a Countess or not, you must first have something to eat, or you will faint.'

So he took me with him to the buffet. I soon forgot the Countess, her words and her emotion, for in Berlin I met a great many persons who conversed amiably with me.

More than four years passed away. On the 4th of August 1890 I was dining with my family in the beautiful villa 'Belvedere,' in Sassnitz. The servant came in and gave me a card, saying that a lady was waiting in the entrance-hall, and that lady was the Countess Schimmelmann. I found that her appearance had greatly improved since our previous meeting. She looked extremely happy and contented, and also fresh and healthy. When we were alone she informed me that ever since that evening in the Architektenhaus she had never ceased to implore God to give her some useful task in His vineyard, be it as lowly as it might. The Lord heard her cry.

Four years before this she had gone to Göhren, her trunk having been sent there by mistake, and remained there for some weeks, although it had originally been her intention to seek a quiet retreat for meditation at Thiessow. At that time she was in deep distress, on account of her father's death, and was passing through great bodily suffering and weakness. Amid the peaceful scenes of Göhren she sought recovery for body and soul. She found what she was in search of, although not in the sea air and in the quiet rest of the woods, but by means of work—delightful, difficult, much derided work among the thousands of fishermen who frequent the place. She invited me to come and see how and where the Lord was using her.

I was deeply moved by her account, although I could not help distrusting it a little. So I resolved to inspect and test her work on the spot, and therefore I went to Göhren on the 7th of August, as I have already mentioned.

What I saw was beautiful beyond all expectation. We will not stand any longer under the flag, but will enter the 'Villa'[1] of the Countess, that lies behind, and hear her talk about her work while we drink a cup of tea with her.

A 'Villa'? Yes, if you like the name; but it is more like a simple country cottage. It contains only four rooms of extremely dwarfish

[1] The 'Villa,' better 'Pavilion,' was built of wood and clay, and was twenty feet by eighteen.—A. S.

dimensions. The largest is the drawing-room. In everything the cultured taste of a lady of rank is apparent. Several small pictures painted by herself adorn the room, and the care and skill with which everything is arranged evinced her deep love of the fine arts. Yet when I remembered that the lady who lived in this tiny cottage had been accustomed from childhood to the highest splendours of Court life, and to luxuries of every kind, and that for several years past she had lived like a Princess of the Imperial house, I was obliged to admit that, viewed from the worldly standpoint, she had sunk in social position as deeply as possible.[1]

The small kitchen, with its white walls and shining utensils, is attached to the drawing-room, but the bedroom was nothing more than a second class cabin. Somewhat longer than this

---

[1] In 1894, to speak with Funcke, I sank still lower than this, for, under the pretext of 'love and care,' I was placed by my relations, who alleged that I had been mad for nine years, in the Sixth Division of the People's Hospital in Copenhagen, where I passed through indescribable sufferings of body and mind among the degraded and deranged inmates. Compared with this my life in the humble 'Pavilion' at Göhren was luxurious.—A. S.

is the fourth room, which may be called the nursery. It contains two beds and a hammock, and is occupied by three poor boys, whose ages range from five to nine years, the sons of drunken Pomeranian fishermen. The boys, once so wild and rude, are now quite tame and gentle, and I am sure every one of them would willingly go through fire and water for the Countess.

That is the 'Villa' and its inmates, and now we sit and drink tea with the Countess. She has prepared it herself, and to-day, in honour of the guest, it is rather strong. The sugar-basin is as small as if it belonged to a doll's tea-set, and many a Bremen tea-drinker would empty its entire contents into his cup. But the Countess, who was now giving all she possessed to her fellow-creatures, and looked for nothing in return, sat there as happy as a queen, and talked to me of the many hundreds of her 'children'—the fisher-men, of whom several during my visit entered to speak with her on matters affecting their welfare. Every one was addressed by name. Question and answer were always in Low German, and even Fritz Reuter himself would have listened with pleasure to the faultless dialect of the Countess on the sandhills of Göhren. She had acquired it in childhood on her father's estate in Holstein, and had never forgotten it. It was of great service to her now. The fishermen are not at home in High German, and in any case Low German speaks more directly to their hearts.

The Countess may now speak for herself.

III

HOW A COUNTESS TAMES BEARS

'THE dwellers along the Pomeranian shore take naturally to a seafaring life, for which, by character and training, they have a marked pre-dilection. They become for the most part fisher-men, although the Navy and the Commercial Marine are largely recruited from their ranks.

'But since the fishing off the shore and in inland waters is let on lease, the fishermen are obliged to engage in large numbers in deep-sea fishing. Their work is difficult and danger-ous, and, while attended with many hardships and deprivations, it barely yields a livelihood. But the men love their work.

'As in winter their occupation is rendered almost impossible, they are obliged to be very diligent from February to November. During this period they rarely come home, and even

then only for a few hours at a time. They live
entirely in their boats, which are of the poorest
description.   Only a few are furnished with a
very small cabin in which the most necessary
provisions and cooking utensils are kept.   The
majority of the boats are quite open.   Their
occupants live and sleep on deck, and are day
and night exposed to the weather.   They keep
their provisions in a wicker basket.   These consist
of bread, fat, and—at least formerly—brandy,
which they consumed in large quantities, and
which they regarded as an alleviation of their
wretchedness, although in reality it depraved
them, and rendered them terribly rude.

‘ In earlier days they were treated with some
degree of kindness when they went ashore.   The
people allowed them to sleep in their barns, and supplied them, at reasonable prices, with potatoes and
other necessaries.   But when one after another the
fashionable watering-places arose, the inhabitants
refused to have anything to do with the rough
strangers.   The canteens alone remained open to
the fishermen, and in these they were fleeced of
their hard-earned wages, and rendered more rude

and brutal. At length these "hordes" of strange fishermen became as deeply hated as they had been feared. They often took by force what was refused them in kindness, dug up the potatoes in the gardens, cut down the wood in the forests, and entered with threatening demands the houses of citizens and peasants. It can hardly be wondered at that they were refused even a drink of water, and that the people did all in their power to scare them from the coast, and to prevent them from landing even at the proper places.

'Such was the state of things which existed when, four years ago, I came to Göhren. My father had recently died, and, in deep sorrow of heart over my great loss, I often about that time visited the south coast of the island. Here, and at the little island of Greifswalder Oie, were the principal anchorages for the fishing-boats. There, on a Sabbath morning, I once saw a troop of fishermen going from house to house politely asking for food, for which they were willing to pay. They had tried, by brushing their clothes and cleaning their boots, to show their respect

D

for the day, but no one would give them food, and they were obliged to go back hungry. In such treatment there seemed to me to be something radically wrong, and I ordered my cook to prepare a large boiler full of potatoes and meat, which they soon emptied. My own dinner was sent to the hungry fishermen, and as up to that time my knowledge of hunger had been only by means of books, the experience was a somewhat painful one.

'After my departure I could not get rid of the thought that I might, and ought to, render some help to this neglected and starving people. So, during the winter, which I spent at my home in Denmark, I made up my mind to establish a home for sailors and fishermen. I had seen how thankful they were for the little I had done for them, and how deeply they were impressed by the interest which a lady of high rank had taken in them. They were astonished at being treated with the love of a mother. Besides this, I noticed that I had gained such influence over these rude men just because I was a lady.

'On taking steps to carry my plan into effect,

I had to encounter strenuous opposition. Some thought me demented; others regarded me as "emancipated" and unladylike in an alarming degree; others again said that I was committing a sort of suicide, for they told me that in such company I should become rough, or at least lose all fine feeling.

'Notwithstanding this, I entered upon the work eagerly and full of good cheer. Naturally the wrath of the tavernkeepers was aroused, and all those who had ill-treated the fishermen threw great difficulties in my way. If the kind Chief-President, and especially President Von Arnim, had not extended to me their protection, my enterprise would soon have failed. There were two taverns in the Greifswalder Oie. In consequence of my activity the owner of one of these had become bankrupt. The second I purchased; but the night preceding the day on which I had arranged to occupy it, it was set fire to and reduced to ashes.[1]

'On the south shore hatred and calumny were

---

[1] It was afterwards rebuilt of clay, and an adjoining stable converted into a kitchen.—A. S.

so rife that I was turned out of the inns with a volley of abuse.[1]

'But God's work still goes on, and its blessing is indescribable. You shall presently see our rooms here in Göhren. On the Greifswalder Oie, where, with our own hands, we have built a simple cottage of clay, I employ a probationer and a cook, who attend to the spiritual and bodily needs of the fishermen. I visit the island frequently, and suffer much from sea-sickness, but that cannot be helped. I am compelled, indeed, to be a real water-rat, as I visit the fishermen's families in the villages on the coast, to assist with advice and practical help. In several villages near the shore I have established reading-rooms, which are heated and lighted every Saturday and Sunday. Here the men like to come to read and write, and to play at dominoes and other games. I also get people to read to them, or do it myself. Both religious and secular books are supplied to them, and in all our homes the day is opened and closed with prayer.

[1] Later on I was driven away a second time.—A. S.

'During the long winter evenings I give chairs and tables to the men to be carved, and prepare the designs myself. But the work is becoming too great for me. I am obliged to recruit my health in winter at my Denmark home. But single-handed I cannot meet the demands of the Mission. The requests for advice and counsel which the men bring to me from morning to night are sufficient to occupy my entire attention, and, without assistance, I shall be unable to meet the demands of the work.

'My financial resources are also inadequate. I am devoting the whole of my small fortune to the enterprise, but this is not sufficient, and I am in danger of incurring a large yearly deficiency. Yet I am sure that He to whom belongs all gold and silver will send me help. There is so much money in the world, and I am praying that God will make some of it available for my work. The late Emperor William I. gave me £25, and the Empress Augusta £15. In Stralsund a bazaar was held for my Mission with a good result. But these are only like drops of water on a hot stone.

'I get no help from those on the island. Indeed, all are against my Mission : the publicans, because their object is to fleece the fishermen ; and the people in general, because they are anxious to get rid of them.

'And yet the results of my humble work are everywhere to be seen. Drunkenness and rudeness are rapidly disappearing. Large numbers of the young men are trying the new way, and even some of the old men are living a changed life. Many are hungering and thirsting after the spiritual food of this heavenly righteousness. In the families of the fishermen here and there an entirely different state of things is apparent. The husbands bring their wages to their happy wives, and peace and joy enter where formerly strife and discord held sway. The grateful tears of the poor wives, who have told me that their husbands are quite changed since they "went to the Countess," are numberless.

'Often in a single day our Sailors' Home at Göhren is visited by hundreds of men who a short time ago were the terror of the neighbourhood, but who now come and go unobserved.

For myself, I can affirm that I have never witnessed a rude scene of any kind among the men, and I have used no means to subdue their rising tempers, except a glance or a whispered word of quiet reproof or entreaty. They call me "Our Mother," although some of them are twice my age. But I prize this title as my highest badge of honour—if only I could more fully deserve it. But now, please, come with me, and let me show you the "Home."'

IV

IN THE SAILORS' HOME

As we left the 'Villa' we were joined by the little fair-haired, blue-eyed boys whom 'Our Mother' had rescued from an immoral and degrading family-life. They were now gentle and quiet, and clung, full of tenderness, to the tall figure of the Countess, as if she were their own mother. The lads were scrupulously clean and neatly dressed, although, like poor fishermen's children, they wore neither shoes nor hats. Like faithful dogs they followed the Countess wherever she went.

From the sand-dune we had a magnificent view far out into the sea, while just below us were groups of fishermen taking observations of wind and weather, and watching the arrival and departure of ships, and the passing of vessels in the far distance.

Not far from the Villa the Countess pointed
out to me a well which she had had sunk. 'You
cannot imagine,' she said, 'how refreshing this
spring water is to the men. During their voyages
they are obliged to drink for weeks together the
brack water of the Baltic.' Near the well stands
a shed, the floor of which is covered with straw.
This is the only sleeping apartment which the
Countess has been able to provide for the fishermen ; but to them, after weeks on the hard deck,
it is a kingly couch. Adjoining the shed is the
Sailors' Home, a large and lofty room, furnished
in simple style, and capable of accommodating
about fifty persons. Here we saw the cook, an
elderly but robust woman of cheerful counten-
ance, and dressed in the becoming costume of the
Mönchgut women.

At the time of my visit the tables were surrounded by some thirty men, from twenty to
sixty years of age. Some were reading or play-
ing at dominoes, others were eating or drinking
or smoking. It was touching to see how respectfully and gratefully these rough sea-bears looked
up to the tall fair lady as she entered. I have

read in old tales how noble, gentle maidens, by
a soft touch of the hand or glance of the eye
have changed wild beasts to lambs. This came
to my mind when I saw how courteously, and
almost reverentially, these rough fishermen, once
so dreaded, behaved towards the Countess. It
was clear that any sacrifice she might ask of
them would be joyfully made.

They gave a cordial welcome to their visitor,
partly, perhaps, because they had already heard
of me. In a kindly manner the Countess presented me to them. The Low German came
softly and graciously from her lips. Her whole
manner with the fishermen was neither patronising nor officious, but full of a true and natural
heartiness. I spoke with the men, who at first
were a little stiff, but by-and-by they became
more communicative. After promising to send
them some good books, I went on to show from
examples which had come under my own notice
that 'godliness is profitable unto all things,
having the promise of the life that now is, and
of that which is to come' (1 Tim. iv. 8).

I observed that the library of the 'Home' had

been carefully selected, and that the little books
which the Countess distributes to the fishermen
for their lonely voyages were well chosen.   I was
obliged to laugh at the immense cups of coffee
supplied to the men, each of which contained a
quart, and cost a little over a farthing.   For
reasons of my own I did not touch the brown
beverage, but I could see how greatly the sailors
enjoyed it, and that is the main thing.

I was then shown the crockery in which dinner
is served to the men.   To each is given a huge
dish of peas or beans with potatoes, and about a
quarter of a pound of bacon for less than two-
pence.   The quantity given would have served
me for at least a week, but these Pomeranians
not infrequently require a second serving.   The
fishermen are allowed to bring their own fish to
be cooked, and are supplied with vegetables at a
small charge.

The impression left on my mind by all that I
saw was that the former Court lady was able, not
only to rule over these sea-bears in love, but also
to attend to their bodily needs.   In the hot
weather they are supplied with lemonade.   No

spirituous liquors of any kind are provided.
The following figures will give some idea of the
extent to which the men avail themselves of the
privileges of the Home. In three and a half
months 5622 plates of warm food were supplied,
and on one day five pails of lemonade and more
than a hundred cups of coffee were consumed.
The number of visitors naturally varies with the
weather and the time of the year; but every man
with eyes to see is compelled to confess that the
Sailors' Home, although consisting of a few
cottages on a sand-dune, is nevertheless the 'city
set on a hill' of which Christ speaks.

Oh how much harm is done, wittingly or in
ignorance, by those who frequent our watering-
places! The greed of gain aroused in the inhabitants by their presence, and the consequent
self-indulgence and immorality of all kinds, seem
inevitable when our small seaside resorts are invaded by wealthy strangers. How many simple
and pious communities have been depraved within
a few years by these evils!

But here I saw with great joy of heart that a
stranger may bring peace and happiness to a

place. I am myself glad that I did not refuse to
speak the other day at the Mission celebration in
the Wald church at Sassnitz, and thus to contribute a salutary influence. In addition, I
formed several good resolutions. I trust my
readers may be led to do the same, and that they
will never in future leave their seaside resort
without having tried to do good to the residents,
and especially to help them on in their way to
heaven. We may well take the Countess as our
example in this respect. Constrained by Divine
love, she gave all she possessed to provide a
home for the homeless fishermen.

OUR RESPONSIBILITY

THE hours passed like a dream. The steam-whistle of the *Rügen* had announced more than once that it was time to leave, and the Countess accompanied me to the shore. On the way we passed some pretty fisher-cottages. Here she spoke a word to a weak old woman, there she caressed a godchild. I was astonished to see how lightly and easily the former Court lady made her way through the deep sand at Göhren. I gave expression to my thought, and she answered, smiling: 'I have only really lived since I began to live for my fellow-creatures. Even physically I am much stronger than in those days, as I am obliged to work from morning to night, and have no time to think so much of my health.' 'He that hath ears to hear, let him hear!' The account I have given is a heart-moving sermon. I will offer no other.

How much work there is to be done in this world! One requires only an eye, a Christian eye, for the sorrows of life, and there will be no need to ask, 'Lord, what wilt Thou have me to do?' How many persons, especially ladies of the so-called 'upper classes,' spend their time amid the fleeting vanities of life weary in body and soul! And yet they could be happy themselves and bring happiness to others if they acted like the Countess. Find your happiness in making others happy. Will not one of my readers say: 'I will do all in my power to help the Countess in her work'?

But do not be in too great a hurry. I would entreat you not to send in your name if you are only desirous of seeing a pious play. Perhaps there is no need to trouble about the matter at all, for I do not expect that too many will offer themselves for the work. Many, indeed, are not required in the two Homes at Göhren and Greifswalder Oie. But the Mission is in urgent need of financial aid, and some who

read this are able to send it, and thus to help,
I do not say the Countess, but Christ Himself.

For it is His work—although, as in the case
of all work intrusted to human hands, it is not
faultless. O reader, do for Christ's sake help!
Those fishermen from the twenty-three Pomeranian
and eight Rügen villages of whom the Countess
takes care at Göhren and at the Oie are assuredly
among those of whom the Lord says: ' Inasmuch
as ye have done it unto one of the least of these
My brethren, ye have done it unto Me '—Me, your
Saviour—Me, the King of kings—Me, the Eternal
Judge.

The sun went down as the *Rügen* weighed
anchor. In the fading light I caught sight of the
white figure of the Countess climbing the dune
with elastic step; the flag saluted once more,
and we steamed round the eastern point of the
island. The sea was flooded with purple light;
the sea-gulls bathed their white breasts in the
cool waves; the wild ducks seemed to throw
themselves into the radiance of the parting day.
On every hand we saw fishing-boats with their
white sails, looking glorified. And indeed, what-

ever comes into contact with the love of Christ is within the sphere of glorification. As I stood on the bridge, land and sea lay beneath me in entrancing splendour.

But a yet lovelier world presented itself to my ' inward vision '—that world in which everything is filled and transfused with the love of Christ For this world my heart yearned, and, longing for it, my eyes filled with tears of homesickness. Need I say why just at this moment I was led to see it so vividly? I could not forget that by men, redeemed men, God in heaven was sweetening the salt waters of the world, for I had seen once more how much one person, single-handed, could do to relieve the needy and the spiritually neglected, if he be but willing to sacrifice himself, and to despise the unreasoning scorn and abuse of the wicked. This self-denial and this courage are alike indispensable, and, because both are so often wanting, our work is, for the most part, ineffectual.

When I thought of the Countess, I felt ashamed —and I trust that many of my readers will feel ashamed—with the shame which is the morning

E

red out of which the sunrise, and many a new creation of loveliness, is born. The world believes in Christ only in so far as it sees the noble deeds, and feels the love, of His followers.

While I was standing there in deep thought, and looking dreamily into the quivering waters, one of the sailors called me out of my reverie: ' Have you been to see the Countess, Herr Pastor? I saw that she came down to the boat with you.'— ·Yes, I have been there,' I answered. ' And now, tell me candidly, what do you think of her Mission?' —' Herr Pastor,' he replied, ' if we listen to what people say, we ought to think the Countess mad. But we, who know how things were before she came, and how different they are now, can only be astonished at the work which one person can do.'

This was a simple but impartial judgment. It contained high praise. Oh yes, but the danger of becoming proud over the results of our work is great.[1]

---

[1] And yet there is little danger, for it is not our might that works, but the power of God. Those who are moved by God's spirit are His children.—A. S.

From this pride we can be preserved as little by the hatred and scorn of the world as by the greatest deprivations which we willingly endure. I am well assured that vanity can exhibit itself not only in a pretty dress, but even 'through a rent in the garment. In every age there have been people who left behind them all they possessed in the world, and lived a hermit life, nourishing themselves like beasts of the desert on the roots of the earth, but who, notwithstanding their sacrifices—nay, even on account of them— were as proud as any Pharisee could well be. Hence am I constrained to pray to God, as, indeed, I do daily, that He may keep from His handmaid all spiritual pride, and leave her in her godly simplicity. It is not easy.

I hear people say, 'It is you who make it difficult for her by bringing her work to the notice of the world in your writings. That consideration received my earnest attention. But the Countess's work has already been made public by those who slander and calumniate her, and who oppose her by all the means in their power. And these are not only canteen-keepers and scoundrels, but also people who are highly esteemed. Then, since material help is so greatly needed, am I not justified in lifting up my voice in behalf of the oppressed and defenceless? As the Bible says: 'Open thy mouth for the dumb.' In doing this I have a good conscience; in remaining silent I should have a bad one. In this work, however, as in every other, we require to give heed to the exhortation, 'Watch and pray, that ye enter not into temptation.'

It was almost dark when the anchor of our steamer rattled into the sea in view of the beautiful Sassnitz. A few moments before, the refrain had reached me of a sweet, familiar song, floating over the waves, and coming nearer and nearer. It came from my dear ones and friends, who were on their way in a small boat to meet me. But no song, sacred or secular, beginning with

'Es steht ein Baum im Odenwald,'

and ending with the mighty

'Ich bete an die Macht der Liebe,'

could keep my heart from wandering back to the lonely and forsaken Countess among her rough fishermen on the desolate sandhill, sharing their joys and sorrows, and with gentle power directing their hearts upward to the eternal Fatherland, the home of the Blessed.

You must get rid of the mischievous German tendency of philosophising and grumbling, and assist us to undo the devil's work on the lovely Pomeranian coast. Not only the blue-eyed toilers in the waters of the Baltic, but even the angels in heaven, would rejoice over the consummation of such an undertaking.

GREIFSWALDER OIE

I

MY ISLAND HOME

IT was some time after the publication of *A Home Abroad* that I first saw it. I did not like it at all at first, and my fishermen felt greatly hurt at being called 'bears.' But afterwards I became thankful for the testimony, because it spared me the necessity of explanation, and gave a very good account of some aspects of my Mission. Some supplementary words are, however, necessary, especially with regard to the work at Greifswalder Oie, where the conditions of success were much more difficult.

Here, in the first year, the buildings connected with my Mission were burnt down, and we had to be content with an old barn, which we repaired ourselves with clay and wood. Our kitchen was an old stable eight feet square, and in this small space we often had to cook for four hundred persons.

During my visit to the island, which was usually from the middle of August until November, when the ice first made its appearance, I lived in a place bearing the proud name of 'Government Apartments,' two very damp rooms, in one of which a flower grew out of the floor, and where stood several chests containing flags. These we were not allowed to use, as they belonged to the German Marine.

All our bread had to be brought from the continent, some twenty miles distant, and we found it difficult to keep it good on account of the extreme dampness of the atmosphere. It occasionally happened, during a violent storm, that large numbers of boats put in at the island; and as at such times it was impossible for a boat to leave the island or for one to reach us from the mainland, we found it very difficult to subsist on our limited supply of provisions. In one instance I was compelled to telegraph for a steamer to come to us with bread, and for a long time it was uncertain whether she would be able to reach us.

On another occasion I went to the continent myself for provisions, and was obliged to return at great risk to life, reaching the island just in time to relieve my starving men.

We sometimes had as many as from three to four hundred fishermen at the Oie at the same time. In the years preceding my arrival, drunken brawls and deadly encounters between the men of rival villages had been of frequent occurrence. Policemen had been sent over to keep order, but they were of little use. They were dependent on the peasants for their food, and consequently winked at the evils arising out of the brandy trade and other irregularities. No fighting took place after my arrival; for, as soon as the boats of a hostile village were seen to be approaching, the fishermen would send and ask me to come personally. We at once prepared coffee in our large boilers, each of which contained five bucketfuls, and I took my place among the men, listening to the accounts of their haul, and telling them anything I thought might interest them. Our talk generally ended with a Bible-lesson, which was made applicable to them and

their peculiar experiences. They greatly enjoyed
the singing of psalms and hymns. Of these we
were provided with a good selection from a
neighbouring village, where an old schoolmaster
had established a singing-class.

The quiet evenings on this little island, in full
view of the setting sun and the green landscape
of the distant continent, were enjoyable beyond
description. Instead of brawls and blasphemies,
the Christian songs of my sunburnt sons of the
sea, as they lay beside their provision-baskets in
the grass or in their boats, sounded far over the
ocean in many-voiced unison. I was accustomed
to sit in the doorway of our old clay barn and
keep a watchful eye on everything within and
without; and yet, dilapidated as was our barn,
the men called it 'our home,' and me 'our
mother.' Yes, with motherly care I loved 'my
fishermen,' as they called themselves. The love
of Christ awoke this feeling in my heart, and I
love them still. *His* words, 'Inasmuch as ye
have done it unto one of the least of these My
brethren, ye have done it unto Me,' opened my
eyes, so that I was able to see a messenger of

Him in every forlorn and sorrowful man and woman I met. When my gold and silver were exhausted, and I was unable to give them material help, in Christ's name I gave, as the Apostle did, the help that is better. Sometimes, I am glad to say, I have received letters from men without home and food asking for 'but a kind word of consolation from "our mother."' They asked me not to send money, because they were anxious not to be a burden to me, and they knew that all my means were devoted to the Mission. They fully understood that the best thing I had to give them was the message I delivered to them, the gospel of my Jesus; and it is my greatest joy to believe that not one of the many thousands of men whom God placed in my way during the nine years I laboured among them can ever think of me without remembering Him for whom and with whom I went in and out among them.

II

SPECIAL CORRESPONDENT

DURING several years the fishermen had little success in their work. Their hauls were very small. Then the lease of the bow-nets, which was settled, was of service to only a few men, and made the lot of large numbers of small net fishermen very hard. The evil became so great that I was compelled to appeal to the Government to help the fishery; and, as I was living on the island, I was asked to assist the Commissioners and the local authorities in their endeavours to get at the source of the distress.

We held meetings, and talked matters over. Many conflicting interests were involved, and—in a word—there are many different ways of catching fish! Unfortunately it was quite impossible for the authorities to bring the fishing-trade under quite so strict a law as is done in the case of everything else in Prussia. The sea and its sons have many things in common, and I hoped that the peculiar character of each would be considered. It was useless, however; for, although the Government took great pains in the matter, it does not seem to be within the scope of the Prussian law to take notice of the changing conditions of the sea and of the seamen. Everything—the sea not excepted—must be controlled by strict military rule!

One of the troubles was that the fishery was not rich enough to support so many men. The nets lay so close together that every spot was fished three times a year, and that is too often. Then the fishermen are born sailors, and it is next to impossible to compel them to give up their seafaring life. In nearly every case in which children have been put to any other calling they have returned to the fishery. Inborn love of the sea is doubtless the chief cause of this remarkable tendency, although it is partly accounted for by the fact that it is most difficult to get remunerative work in any other direction in Pomerania. The landlords have their own farm-labourers, and labour of all kinds is badly paid.

Consequently the fishermen are very poor. Where there are visitors to a watering-place things are somewhat better. There are, however, many families of from seven to ten persons that have neither house nor land, and are obliged to subsist on from £15 to £20 a year. In the summer they live on fish, in the winter on salt herrings and potatoes, which they earn by working for the peasants.

They drink black chicory-water, a beverage which they call 'German coffee,' and which, like other specimens of that mixture, was very far from being palatable. One man is able to take five of our huge cupfuls of this nauseous drink to his breakfast, which generally consists of bad rye-bread and fat. In the poorest families the fat is often absent. Nay, in the winter season, some families cannot even procure bread, so that they are obliged to live on herrings, potatoes, and chicory-water.

My readers will now see how necessary it was from time to time to give a nourishing dinner

SEAMEN'S HOME, GÖHREN

to these men, free of charge, in the Sailors' Home. Coffee was always supplied to them for nothing, and, in the summer, a sort of lemonade. In the height of the fishing season we generally gave out, in the course of an afternoon, from seven to fourteen bucketfuls of lemonade, and from five to nine of coffee. The poorest of the fishermen are those who engage in the herring fishery, and anything that is done for the improvement of the fishery seems only to serve the interests of the fishmongers and the other fishermen. On one occasion Count Caprivi sent a messenger to me. The members of the Government often visited me at Göhren, and took me with them to the Greifswalder Oie. On one occasion all the members of the Government came down, from the Premier, and the Minister of Fisheries, to the members of the local government.

As I had been advised of their visit, I was able to summon my fishermen from the principal villages, and prepare them for the occasion. Although feeling far from well myself, we held a meeting which lasted until midnight.

F

The points on which I insisted were, that they should not contradict one another in their evidence, and that everything said before the Court should be reported. But when some of the fishmongers at the Oie heard that a proposal for the payment of duty on Swedish herrings was to be brought forward, they circulated a report that a telegram had been received to the effect that the steamer conveying the officials would not arrive until the evening. The men were consequently led to believe that they had ample time to cast their nets before its arrival, and when I came upon the scene I had the mortification of finding that all the men, with the exception of a few clever ones, had left the nest. In the afternoon they returned quite perplexed—they had met the steamer returning from the island !

This led me to inform them that I had resolved not to take an active part in the business affairs of the fishery in future. The two villages whose representatives had wisely remained behind secured important concessions—to one a grant of ten tuns of land on easy terms for each fisher-

man was promised, and to the other the con-
struction of a harbour. My communications with
the Government in behalf of the men were so
numerous that my handwriting had become
known at headquarters. My conveniences for
writing were somewhat limited. I used for a
desk a herring-tub covered with a piece of
board, and a large stone for a seat. As some
of my documents came before the Parliament,
and passed through many hands, I was brought
into direct correspondence with several leading
officials of the state at Berlin. This kind of
work was not greatly to my liking, and, besides
taking me away from my Mission, it made too
great a demand upon my time. I therefore
gradually gave it up, and, in order to free
myself entirely from the burden, I determined
to absent myself for a year. Other weighty
reasons led me to take this step.

III

BRANDY AND EVIL SPIRITS

DURING the winter months, when nothing was being done at the fishery, I used, in the earlier years of my Mission, to make tours among the towns and villages for the purpose of taking care of the fishermen's wives and children, and the young people generally. The schools were always open to me, and the clergymen were glad of my presence and co-operation. At first the small taverns were open to me, and in these I lodged during my visits, but afterwards I was obliged to seek lodgings elsewhere, as the innkeepers became my bitterest enemies. Several of them were reduced to bankruptcy because the fishermen learned to do without beer and brandy, and ceased to be their customers. The opposition to my work arose principally, I believe, from this quarter. In Germany, political opposition of any kind invariably allies itself with beer and brandy; the taverns are the ordinary meeting-places for everything connected with it. The publicans took me probably for the cause of every misfortune, and did their best to set the people against me. Although sometimes exposed to imminent danger on account of their ill-will, I was delivered from all the evil they devised against me. The worst thing that happened to me was to get a basin of water thrown over my head. I am not naturally timid, and my great comfort was to know that I was continually under the Divine protection.

I will mention only one instance. Evil influences were often at work in our Sailors' Homes when I was not present, and on the occasion I refer to a well-concerted plan to injure my work had been laid. A former innkeeper, together with a student who had failed in his college course, a few socialistic workmen, and some peasants at the Oie, who were angry at having lost the profits arising from the sale of strong drink, persuaded the man whom I had engaged to manage the 'Home' to break our rules by selling brandy. On my return to the Oie the matter was mentioned to me, and I dismissed the manager. On leaving he took all our provisions and furniture with him to an adjoining farm before I was able to prevent him. There I stood, with nothing to give to the seventy hungry fishermen who surrounded me! They then tried to incite the fishermen against me, but we sat down and sang hymns. I vowed not to touch a single morsel until I had procured food for my hungry men, and I urged them not to drink the brandy which was offered to them for nothing. One large kettle had been left behind. The fishermen broke up a bench for fuel, and boiled a kettleful of water. Into this I poured half a dozen bottles of wine which had been intended for the sick, and the men divided the little bread they had in their baskets.

While this was going on I had sent a boat to the mainland with £20 for the purchase of provisions. There raged a storm which made it impossible for an ordinary boat to sail, and there was great rejoicing in the enemy's camp. I was, however, perfectly composed, relying on God's help. Contrary to their expectation I had been

able to persuade a larger boat to put out, manned
by some of the most daring of my sailors. I
remained with the men until late at night, as I
was unwilling to leave them until I was sure
they were asleep, and that there would be no
further disturbance. Before five o'clock the
next morning I was again on the spot, and
was thankful to find that a favourable wind
had furthered my plans. The boat soon arrived ;
and, before the enemy were able to lead my poor
starving children into temptation, we had cooked
in our new kettles one of the best meals they
had ever enjoyed.

The plan having utterly failed, some of these
evil men met in a little wood to attack me on
my way home. By some means, however, I
passed their hiding-place unobserved, and they
did not catch sight of me until I was entering
my room. I was quite alone, with the exception of the two little boys, who were asleep on
the sofa. Singularly, the door-key was not to
be found ; but it did not seem to occur to my
persecutors when they came up to try the door,
very likely believing it to be locked as usual ; they

contented themselves with striking it and making
hideous noises. The windows of my room were
very low, and I presently heard one of the band
propose to his companions that they should
force their way through them. I had with me
a little revolver, which I kept as a keepsake. I
drew back the curtains, placed the lamp on the
table, and loaded the revolver. When the
besieging party saw that I awaited them, revolver in hand, they had the good sense not
to advance. Their anger found vent in clamour
and abuse, and when a number of newly arrived
fishermen came upon the scene they retired
in haste.

I was often exposed to such and even greater
dangers, but it was never the fault of my fishermen. The influence of the Socialists rapidly
increased, and a proclamation was published in
my name, but entirely without my knowledge,
describing my Mission as an anti-Socialistic move-
ment, and calling upon the people to stand by
me. But the mission of my life is to bring souls
to Jesus, and to help my fellow-creatures wherever I can. I knew nothing of the proclamation,

which afterwards brought me much unnecessary trouble. Two years ago the Government
at Stralsund declared that the state of things
at the Oie rendered it necessary that I should
have a male protector, and greatly against my
will, although at last with my consent, they sent
a 'Christian Brother.' This man at first looked
forward to a pleasant sojourn on the island; but
after going about like a martyr for two months,
he declared the position to be unworthy of his
education. I told him I did not think it unworthy of mine, and very gladly returned to the
old state of things. The 'Christian Brethren,'
at least some of those belonging to the Institutions of that body in North Germany are con-
ceited on account of the smattering of pedagogic
knowledge which they acquire without proper
education.

IV

MY BOYS

LATER on I was asked by the authorities if I
was not aware of the prevalence of anarchistic
agitations, and was offered one or two *gen-
darmes* for my personal protection.   I thanked
them, and said that I had my own bodyguard.
I had secured one without intending it in the
following way.   For some time previously I had
had the work in the 'Homes' done by grown-up
lads instead of girls, who for obvious reasons were
not suitable for the position.   This suggested to
me the idea of using the 'Homes' for the training and protection of boys who had been confirmed.   The idea worked well, although I must
confess that it required almost infinite patience.
I have had over a dozen of these lads in the
'Homes,' and most of them turned out well.
About the same time I purchased my yacht,

the *Dove*, for the purpose of carrying provisions, and to enable me to visit the villages;
and I used it also as a sort of training-ship for
the boys, under a trustworthy mate.

My boys were in many cases wild and difficult
to manage; but if I had once won their confidence, gratitude, and love, I was able to train
them. If Christ's love is taught in word and
deed it is a power able to soften and subdue
the wildest heart. Most of ' my boys,' as they
were called, had no other home, and whenever,
later on, they returned on furlough or without
situation, they came to me. My aim was to get
them places in the marine, and give them a good
start in life; and I was greatly affected when
one of them once said to me: ' I won't be entirely
converted, because then you will at once say,
" Please make room for the next one who
wishes to be converted," and then "Home " and
" mother " will be gone.' Then I felt that if I
had ever begun to be a 'mother' to a homeless
heart, I could never leave it again.

I have therefore tried to keep in touch with
each one, and my door is always open to them,

wherever I am, if they return to me prosperous or repentant after their wanderings. Such a training is not an easy thing to undertake, but I understand that a human life which has been reared amid degrading surroundings needs the patience of many years to wholly deliver it from the stamp of evil.

If you can induce such a lad to be candid there is good hope, and he will soon give up his vices. The outward roughness can only be slowly subdued. I must add that none of these lads, however bad they were when they first came to me, ever stole, or drank, or ran off secretly into evil society so long as they were with me. In the hours of recreation, and especially in the evening, I did all I could to make them happy, and I generally stayed with them myself.

V

OTTO AND WILLIE

BESIDES 'my boys' I have my 'own little boys,' little twins who are now eleven years of age, and whom I adopted five years ago. Their names are Otto and Willie. I was asked to adopt them by the people of the village in which I was living at the time, and Otto joined his entreaties with theirs, and implored me to take him with me. Otto was at that time almost mad. The sinews of his neck had been cut, and his ribs badly injured, so that he was deformed and in very delicate health. We did not expect him to live. Willie had lost a piece of his skull, which left an open wound. He was an idiot. Of the treatment which had reduced them to their sad condition I cannot now speak. Most of those who saw them regarded them with a pitiful loathing. God knows how much trouble

and pain they gave me day and night. At first
I did it for Christ's sake, but afterwards I grew
to love them for their own sakes, until my gay,
clever, little lads became the sunshine and joy
of my lonely heart.   It is only human that I
became a little proud of them.   I love them now,
as a mother loves her children.   In spite of the
utter neglect in which they had been brought up,
they remained wonderfully pure and innocent
for their age.   As they required an exceptional
education, adapted to their condition, I did not
send them to school, but had them privately
taught according to the advice of well-known
teachers and physicians.   There is much of
deep and almost tragic interest connected with
their earlier years, and with a later terrible
episode in my own life.   Very much also of a
pleasing character would I like to narrate of
their trust in the Saviour and their devotion to
His service, but for the present I must forbear,
and close my brief notice of them with the remark that they—these delicate little twins,—or,
occasionally one or two of the larger boys, were
my 'bodyguard.'

AMONG BERLIN SOCIALISTS
AND ANARCHISTS

I

WHY I WENT TO BERLIN

I HAD to pass through Berlin on my way to Denmark to visit my mother for the last time as she lay dying. About that time a society was being organised, professedly to support my work. An announcement was issued in my name, and a committee was convened which promised me help to the extent of £250 yearly. They urged me to spend more for my own comfort, but asked me to advance £300 for the current year, which I did with pleasure. They failed that year and also the following year to pay the amount promised, although they had raised large sums of money, and they then conceived the idea of making the 'Homes' self-supporting. I was to promise not to spend my own money, and to give nothing in the 'Homes' without payment; beer was to be sold to

G

meet the expenses. I replied that I was prepared to render an account of the £250, if I
should receive it; that what I myself gave was
a matter that did not concern the committee;
but that a beer-house I could not keep! In
connection with these affairs, and to visit some
friends, I went to Berlin the next year. As I
have already mentioned, I resolved to sever my
connection with those affairs of the fishery
which did not directly concern me, by leaving
the islands for a time; and as I had received
an invitation to visit Berlin in order to discuss
matters of importance with a Secretary of State
who had previously called on me at Göhren, I
went to the capital. I was, moreover, desirous
of seeing Chancellor Caprivi, who himself had
given me assistance.

II

THE GOSPEL AND HARD WORK

AT that time there was great misery among the unemployed of the capital. The demon of hunger was rampant. No religious restraints checked the passions or soothed the sorrows of the poor. In the northern portion of the city, where the congestion was most keenly felt, the town mission was beginning, twenty years too late, to care for the people. The clergy were unable to gain the attention of the infuriated mob, and it was deemed necessary to protect their lives by prohibiting their meetings. I can speak of these meetings from observation, as I attended the last that was held. I was accompanied by the Countess Z—— (daughter of the Minister of Religion[1]). I had met with rough men in connection with my work among the sailors, but I had never before seen conduct like that which prevailed at the meeting.

[1] The Cultus Minister.

Although they would not listen to the clergyman, those who stood near were willing to hear us. This was to me the beginning of a winter of hard work.

At first a dozen starving men came to hear more about Jesus—some of these are now good workmen and out-and-out Christians—and day by day the number grew larger. Where was I to accommodate them? No Christian hotel would allow them to come, for did they not come out of the notoriously wicked parts of the city? We were lent a room at the Young Men's Christian Association; but even this, after two days, we were requested to leave. Then the Moravians lent us their church for three days, and our numbers greatly increased.

It was necessary to find something to do for all these men, who had wives and children, aged parents, and little brothers and sisters starving at home.

Some of my friends expressed a wish to buy specimens of the carved furniture which I had taught my fishermen to make. I therefore got the unemployed carpenters to make them, and

taught other men to carve them.   Others, again,
supplied the brass-work, and painters and polishers
added the finishing touch.   By this means all the
men got a share of the profits.   My friends liked
the furniture, and ordered more.   The Moravians,
however, required their church, which we could
not possibly have converted into a workroom.
The hungry workmen nearly stormed the doors
in the hope of getting a little work or food.

Here let me say that the men, for the most
part, preferred to receive their wages in the form
of food, which they could take to their families.
I was constrained, therefore, to hire a room
on my own account, in which about fifty of
them could sit and work.   From morning to
night I was with them myself; indeed, with the
exception of the Countess Z——, I was the only
one who could keep order among them.   I tried
to devolve this duty upon clergymen, missionaries,
and other ladies, so that I might attend to other
forms of work ; but it was useless.   The moment
my back was turned, the room became a pande-
monium, and noisy scenes, like those which I had
seen at the last meeting of the city mission, were

enacted. To me they were as obedient as children, and never, when I read or explained the Bible to them, have they interrupted me in an improper manner. On the contrary, they listened with the deepest interest. I often saw tears in their eyes in cases in which I should least have expected them. They asked questions on points which they did not understand, and in this way our Bible readings gave me opportunities for the most personal conversation with them on spiritual things.

The majority of the men in my workshop took a pride in denying the existence of God and their possession of a soul. 'First let me see the Fellow, and then I will believe in Him,' is a common-place blasphemy among the Berlin workmen. But how much injury have they suffered at the hands of Christians during long years of neglect! If the Churches had considered in time that these thousands of despised men have immortal souls which are as precious in God's sight as those of the greatest magnates of the Church, they would never have refused to believe in their own higher nature and in Him who gave it to them. They had been treated as soulless work-machines; can one wonder that they were led to doubt the truth of the gospel preached by their depreciators? Never shall we be able to convince them of the being of God, and of their own high nobility in God's eyes, until we ourselves are so penetrated and filled with the love of Christ that it will be our highest aim to win our meanest brethren for Christ, and until we are willing to sacrifice ourselves wholly in love for them.

A little later on, when I had enlarged my mission, and had gathered hundreds of the unemployed around me,—there were vagabonds and criminals among them,—a police-officer one day entered the workshop and said with astonishment: 'Do you not know, Countess, that you are in the midst of a set of men over whom no power on earth has any control? How is it that you are able to make them sit and work here as quietly as lambs?' I had just been drawing designs on the hard wood from which our furniture was made, and my fingers were bleeding freely, for I had been trying to provide work for fifty carvers. I thought this a good

opportunity of speaking a word in season to
the officer; so, showing him my hands, I said:
'If we can only let these men see that we
love them to the point of sacrificing ourselves
for them, they will then believe in the sacrifice
of the Son of God on the Cross for their redemption, and, seeing the power of His love
in us, they will accept His gospel.'   My visitor,
who had probably never yet thought about
these things himself, seemed to feel the power
of the gospel.   His eyes filled with tears, and
as he went away he shook hands with me
in a way that gratified my heart, although it
did not tend to improve the condition of my
wounded fingers.

EXPELLED

ALL went well, until my workmen began to sing hymns. Our landlord had laughingly permitted all the noise and hubbub which they made on the stairs during the breakfast-hour. But our first and only attempt to hymn the praise of God was too much for him. He told us we must quit. We had sung the hymn beginning:

'Lobet den Herrn, den mächtigen König der Ehren,
   Lob' ihn, O Seele, vereint mit den himmlischen Chören,'

and an old clergyman, who had formerly tried in vain to gain the ear of these men, cried out when he heard them: 'Are you really the same men? You, who once lived such lives, do you now sing the praises of God?' Our landlord, however, was indignant, and when we returned the next morning we found the room locked, and were forbidden to take the furniture which we had made. My poor *protégés* stood around me in the snow, cold and hungry. I was in great distress, and cried, with all my heart, to God for help. Was it possible that, in so large a city, no small room could be found in which I could speak to these men of Jesus, and enable them to earn their living? Difficult as I found it, I took a cab, and went at once to the police-station. I did not mind the astonished looks with which on every hand I was received. I went straight to the officer in charge, and lodged my complaint; but he did not think he would be justified in interfering. Then, just as a higher officer entered, an old policeman ventured, in defiance of all Prussian police etiquette and rule, to make the remark: 'Can you not send one of us to help the lady in the interests of her good work? We have seen what she has been able to do in the streets.' Upon this, the higher official ordered him to accompany me. The sight of a police-man was quite enough for our landlord. He at once opened the room, and put our furniture out in the street! More he would not do. Our case was now almost as desperate as before, but I continued to cry to God for help. There were souls willing to listen to the gospel, and to come to Jesus, *and room* MUST *be found for them.* Then, by a wonderful train of circumstances, God came to our help, and within an hour I was lodged with my band of workmen in first-rate quarters in one of the best streets in Berlin. Mr. Schmidt, a kind-hearted landlord, placed at my disposal a large workroom, a cellar, a little parlour for myself, and a shop in which we could sell our furniture. May God reward him! He little knows how many lives have been relieved and how many souls have been blessed through his timely aid.

I must now ask my readers to leave the workmen sitting beside their huge coffee-pot and a basket of rolls, and go with me to another part of the city.

IV

A HUNGRY MOB

NOT many days after the riotous meeting of the
City Mission, which I attended shortly after my
arrival in Berlin, I arranged with the Countess
Z—— and some other ladies to visit the notorious
northern division of the city, and speak to some
of the men we had seen at that meeting. Our
intention was to meet them in the same hall.
The winter was an exceedingly bitter one, and
the distress was intensely acute. Large numbers
of the unemployed and those dependent on them
were in sore want of food. Nobody, however, seemed to pay any heed to this alarming
state of things. Individual citizens, we may
charitably suppose, regarded the destitution as
so great as to make it impossible for them to
interfere. When I was on the point of driving to
the place appointed for the meeting, I received a

letter from a member of the Government warning me against going, and informing me that the whole neighbourhood was in an uproar. Thereupon the Countess Z—— declined to go. I did not believe that the case was so hopeless, and resolved to carry out my intention. I was unwilling to miss this opportunity of helping these men, who seemed to be on the verge of despair and to have lost all faith in their fellows. My friends made me promise not to go alone, but they would not accompany me. A young student, who was a member of the Young Men's Christian Association, was the only one who volunteered to go. I do not even know his name, but I now tender him my thanks. In addition to him, one of my little eight-year-old foster-sons went with me.

As we approached the proscribed region we met large bodies of men, roaring like wild beasts, and swaying hither and thither like waves in a stormy sea. The place of meeting was still some distance off, and at every step the streets became more crowded, until it was quite impossible to turn. Carriages were overturned, and the unfortunate occupants of a cab, which had been upset, were beaten about the head as they were trying to creep out of the windows. They were carried away bleeding and wounded, but whether dead or alive I could not ascertain. Shop windows were smashed, especially those of provision stores. Hungry men quarrelled for the bread which they had taken from a baker's shop. It was commonly reported in the respectable parts of the city that the unemployed had wilfully trodden the bread under foot, and that their aim in looting the shops was to make a disturbance. The report was utterly false. That some waste occurred in the struggle which took place for the bread there can be no doubt. But to say that the men were not hungry was, unhappily, a pure fiction. The mob became increasingly violent, breaking all the windows that came in their way, and taking whatever they could lay their hands on. When we came near to the place of meeting, we found ourselves in the midst of a surging crowd. Our cab was stopped, and threatening fists were thrust in at the windows. The cry was raised: 'Overturn the cab! Crush it! Why should they drive in a cab when we are starving?'

I afterwards learned that they were in the very
act of raising the cab when I alighted.

I was lifting up my heart to God for these poor
souls, whom men had abandoned, and who themselves had abandoned God. Never before had I
seen such brutal rudeness, and never before had
I felt such burning pity. My soul was so filled
with compassion that there was no place left
for fear. They might have torn me to pieces for
the privilege of being allowed to bring to them
the gospel of Christ's redeeming blood, and to
entreat them to come back to His arms of love.
In that moment I understood how it was that
the martyrs had died without fear. In that
moment, also, I seemed to understand the
meaning of the Apostle's words : 'For this cause
ought the woman to have power on her head
because of the angels.' Instead of referring, as
some theologians say, to a mere head-dress, does
it not mean that a woman who has given herself
wholly to the Lord, is, just on account of her
womanhood and the heavenly grace given to her,
encircled with a power which renders her fit to
assist the angels in their work ?

In the meantime, my little boy had sprung from the cab, and innocently asked one of those nearest to us: 'Why do you shout like this?' A loud voice answered: 'Because we are hungry!'—'But,' replied the child, 'you do not in this way get anything. If you would only come to Jesus Christ, He is rich and can give bread to you all.' The clenched fist of the enraged man was raised over the child's head. The blow, had it fallen, would have killed him. I saw it, and lifted up my heart to the Lord. Whether the hand was restrained by others, or whether the man himself withdrew it, I am unable to say; but it did not fall, and the boy continued, unperplexed and fearless, to speak of Jesus, and to give away some little books which I had put into his pocket. 'Out of the mouth of babes and sucklings hast Thou ordained strength because of Thine enemies; that thou mightest still the enemy and the avenger.'—(Psalm viii. 2).

The scene which presented itself to me when I left the cab defies description, and left an impression on my mind which time will never efface. It will be understood if I simply say that some of the physiognomies which glared upon us were like those of enraged wild beasts, and that others of those human beings, lost to all moral feeling, were excited by passions which degraded them to a level far lower than that of the brute creation.

There were others, however, who made a deeper impression upon my mind. Would that those who are able to help could have seen them! Their faces were deathly pale, and bore an expression of dumb despair. I asked a group of these if it was true that they were hungry, and a tall man with a long black beard directed my attention to a band of noisy young fellows, and said : 'Not those who shout the loudest are the most hungry. We are starving fathers of families. I have six hungry children.' 'I four,' said a second. 'And I five,' added a third. Their pale, haggard faces, the tears in their eyes, and their trembling voices, testified that they were speaking the truth.

I could not restrain my tears, and in that moment the cold distrust and gloomy despair seemed to vanish from their faces. I distributed to them all the money I had with me, and received warm thanks. Our cabman, who was touched with pity, offered to lend me his money, but that was only as a drop in a bucket. I had nothing more to give, but they had seen my goodwill, and the deep pity which they saw I felt for them constrained them to listen, full of confidence, to my words of comfort.

I told them of Him who is the wellspring of love, and whose Divine power alone was able to deliver them from their temporal and spiritual destitution. Their hearts seemed deeply moved as I spoke. · The word of God calmed the uproar, even as the voice of Christ stilled the storm on the lake, and for hours I stood speaking to them and consoling them. Other gangs of men as they passed by and saw the cab and a lady standing beside it would cry out, 'Overturn the cab! Tread her under your feet!' But they were always answered, 'Be silent! Don't touch her! She is good to us! We will hear what she says.'

V

REFLECTIONS

AT another time I may relate in greater detail the events of that terrible night. Despite the tumult of the streets, and the fact that the police had prohibited the meeting, I had effected my purpose, and had been able to speak to several thousands of the unemployed. On our return home our cab was escorted by many of those whom I had addressed.

As we approached the well-to-do parts of the city, the crowds diminished, and mounted police were more frequently to be seen, until, by-and-by, we met whole divisions of them.

Then we reached the neighbourhood of the aristocracy, where perfect tranquillity reigned. Without hindrance my cab drove away at full pace. On passing the royal palace, I looked up at the illuminated windows of the mansion in which I had taken part in many a brilliant festival, at a time when the star of the Imperial House shone most brightly.   In those days I had no idea of the widespread poverty and distress with which the world is filled.

One splendid carriage after another was passing the portals of the palace.   It was said there was a masquerade.   Did all those fashionable people know as little of the needs of their poor brethren, and of their duty towards them, as I in those earlier days?   If they could have had a glimpse of the human hell which I was then leaving, it would have marred their enjoyment! May God have mercy on them!   I had just seen the prophecy of the trouble which their ignorance or indifference might some day bring upon them.

On my arrival at our comfortable, brightly lighted Christian hotel, I met a group of ladies, professing Christians, who told me they had just been to the theatre, and had seen a touching drama depicting the misery of the unemployed!   They urged me to go—the play was really worth seeing!

Deeply affected by all I had seen and heard, I longed for consolation, and thought to find it in a large saloon, where a well-known clergyman was giving a Bible-reading at evening prayer. He entered into an elaborate explanation as to why Jesus on His entry into Jerusalem had sat upon the colt of the ass, and not upon the ass. Thought and feeling and memory rendered it impossible for me to listen to the discourse, and I left the saloon before evening prayer began. This I offered in my room alone, weeping bitterly.

PERSECUTION AND PRISON

I

DIFFICULTIES

THE foregoing pages are mere outlines of mission work, which might be filled in with incident and detail of blessing, extending to volumes. But as this is not only to be an account of my mission work, I must now resume the narration of my further experiences, which will, alas! lead me through scenes of gloom, and even into eclipse of darkness. In no century since the Apostolic age have the forces of light and darkness been opposed with such deadly hostility as they are in the times in which we live. The Acts of the Apostles — let us rather say of the Holy Ghost—are being repeated ; and the penalty— the glory of persecution, the crown of martyr- dom—which they paid is being exacted from Christ's witnesses in the mission-fields of heathenism, and even in lands on which the light of the gospel once shone so resplendently. 'Ye must through much tribulation enter the Kingdom.' We have counted the cost, and, in view of vanishing fortunes and fading crowns, we are making our way by patient endurance of Divinely permitted trials to a place in the Kingdom which cannot be shattered, and to 'an inheritance incorruptible, and undefiled, and that fadeth not away' (1 Peter i. 4).

With the arrival of the spring of 1892 I was able to close my Berlin workshops, as I had succeeded in getting other work for nearly all my men; and I was also able to stop the distribution of relief with a lighter heart as the unemployed generally had for the most part obtained employment. Many of them became true Christians, and quite recently (in 1895) one of them turned up in Hamburg, a well-to-do joiner. My purse and my strength were alike exhausted, so that I was obliged to recruit my energies and husband my resources by retiring for a few weeks' rest to my house on the banks of the Oresund in Denmark. After entertaining some lady friends, and using a part of my

house as a home for several young lads whom I
had rescued in Berlin and could not leave behind
there, I returned to my fishermen in Pomerania,
taking these lads with me to serve in the yacht
I had purchased, or in my Homes. Several of my
unemployed *protégés* in Berlin had found their
way to Göhren, and had taken refuge in the
Home. I gave them work as best I could, and
they served me well. Some of them became men
of excellent Christian character.[1]   So far as I was
able, I kept up communication with the Berlin
men after I had resumed my work in the Baltic.

Conditions of work differ greatly in England
and Germany, and my position as a lady-pioneer
of mission work exposed me to great persecution.
The work effected by German ladies is generally
done by proxy and in connection with public
institutions in which they only take a patronising
interest.   For any lady to engage in public work
directly in the way in which it is so largely done
in England and America is regarded as an un-
pardonable breach of the social proprieties.   I
felt, however, that God wanted *me*, my body and

[1] I have had Danish, German, Swedish, and English boys.

soul, my hands and feet, my eyes and ears, but, above all, my lips, with all my powers of thought and feeling for the proclamation of the good news of salvation, to be directly devoted to His service. There is only one way in which a lady of rank is allowed to do real Christian work. Put on a white cap and place your spiritual life and your individuality under the absolute direction—not of Christ, but—of a Deaconess-Clergyman, and the only sphere permissible to Christian women-workers is open to you! As I felt no call to serve my fellow-creatures under conditions so slavish, and as I had resolved to follow the leadership of Christ alone, I claimed my right to serve God as He should guide me, to fight for and to follow Him, if even through persecution.

Now, however, the enemies of my work became more daringly hostile. Several times they tried to put fire under the floor of my sleeping apartment in the poor wooden 'Pavilion' at Göhren. Only the vigilance of my boys protected me To these, as well as to myself, numerous anonymous letters, warning us of all sorts of difficulties that would befall us, had been sent. The burden

of a later letter was : 'A devilish trap is being
laid to catch you alive, to remove you from your
work, and cause you to disappear.' At the time
we regarded this as an idle threat.

In spite of the fact that many of these warnings had come true, I did not believe the last-
named to be possible. The idea of being 'caught
alive and made to disappear' seemed to me
absurdly wild. And yet, knowing something of
the forces at work against me, I did not doubt
that *some* intrigue was on foot to injure my
mission, if not my person.

I wondered if in any quarter the aims of my
mission could be so grossly misunderstood as to
lead some one to set political intrigues on foot
against me. Some newspapers had represented
it as an agitation in favour of one of the
political parties in the state. I had such influence over the fishermen that at a word from
me they would have voted according to my
advice. But I was a Christian ambassador, and
my politics were not carnal but spiritual.

Then it was suggested, and did seem possible
to me, that the Anarchists believed me to have

gained possession of some of their secrets through my work among their disciples in Berlin, from whence I received many warning communications.

But never for a moment did I guess that the snares were being laid by those who, by every tie of nature, should have been my protectors. Nevertheless I worked on, and my work was blessed. At this juncture came the financial difficulty already mentioned. A reflex light on this matter seems necessary. Committees have not infrequently been a hindrance to the work of individual servants of God who have been called upon to labour under peculiar conditions. The committee mentioned had two faults: it was large, and it was composed of units whose ideas were fundamentally at variance with my own. It was formed at the suggestion of Christian friends who had begun to collect for my mission. They issued circulars asking for contributions in my name, and received a large sum. Of this sum not a penny has been handed to me, although, at the request of the committee, I extended my work and thrice advanced £300, which they promised to refund. At length the committee disagreed, and,

unhappily, my friends left it. Those who remained
sent a deputation to me, demanding that I should
give up my 'Homes' to them, or they would not
pay me a shilling. To this I objected, as the
committee included unconverted Jews in its
number, and had determined to convert the
'Homes' into beer-houses. I did not surrender
the 'Homes,' as I could never allow people who
were not Christians to rule them, and I stood
firm. Then another trouble arose. The cholera
was raging in Hamburg, and Germany was in
a state of panic. Many had fled to the Island
of Rügen, and the inhabitants of its numerous
fashionable resorts were reaping a rich harvest
from their visitors. Every precaution was taken,
and residents and visitors deemed themselves
secure—when, to my great sorrow, the pestilence
appeared in my own establishment! One of my
children had been to the opposite shore in a
fishing-boat, and in the night he fell to the floor
screaming and rolling in his agony. I treated
him in accordance with a lecture I had recently
heard, and sent all my people out of the cottage
into the 'Home.' The doctor declared it to be

cholera, and requested me in the name of the Government to close my ' Homes.' I asked that the authorities would announce in the papers that the 'Homes' were being closed by their order, as I did not wish my fishermen to think that it was being done on my initiative.

The news spread like wildfire, and from the watering-place nearest to us forty carriages full of terrified visitors drove down to catch the next train. The rage of the people was turned against us as the cause of the loss of their gains. We were asked by the doctor to leave the island as soon as the death or recovery of our little patient would permit us to go. The reason they alleged was that they would be unable to protect us against the fury of the people should there be other cases of cholera. My friends, my maid, every one fled from me, and I was left alone in the little cottage on the sandhill, with my child half dead and no provision or assistance at hand. No, not quite all left me ! Two of my boys came to me from the ' Home,' and said : 'We should be worse than villains if we forsook you at such a time. We will stay !' Without them we should have perished, since we were forbidden to go near the village, and none of the inhabitants would come and fill our baskets, although they were washed with carbolic and placed half a mile from the cottage.

Confronted by this serious state of affairs, my boys armed themselves with heavy sticks, and took with them baskets and basins and money. When they came near to the village, the people would have attacked them, had they not been afraid of the infection and the sticks. The boys told them that they were determined to fight their way to the provisions in the shops, and take what they needed 'to save the Countess and the sick child from starving.' The people fled before the advance of my 'light brigade,' and very soon we had sufficient food to supply our needs for a week. Ample payment was left behind. Twice I thought the child was dead, but he recovered, and at the earliest moment I sent for my little ship and went on board. My cholera patient was Otto.

Eight weeks we kept on board the little ship, until all danger of infection was past, and then I went to see a friend of mine, a niece of

I

Bismarck. While there, the warnings which reached me by letter and even directly from people who had reason to be grateful to me, began to grow more and more earnest, so that—although neither believing nor realising the full force of it—(I just laughed at the idea that my youngest brother should be able to do me harm, or, as it was reported, to catch me and cause me to disappear)—my friends and I came at length to believe that there really was some deliberate scheme on foot against me. The proofs of it were in some instances suggested to us; but we were at a loss to guess the real truth, and even, as I now know, sometimes guessed wrongly, because I was unwilling to seek the originators of it in my own family. Having contracted a severe cough, and longing for rest, I decided to go to the south, and some friends of influence urged me to take with me one of the boys who had stood by me so nobly in the hour of need. On my consenting, they asked him to keep a good watch over me.

I was desirous of taking with me my two small foster-children for the sake of their health; and

resolving to do this, and wishful at the same time
to save as much money as I could for my mission,
I travelled most of the journey third-class. That
I might not scandalise my family, as well as for
peace and quietness' sake, I travelled *incognito.*

I was anxious to see some renowned Christian
Faith-healing Homes, as during my mission
work I had had many wonderful experiences in
that department of service. Although the plan
my friends had arranged for my journey was
somewhat uncommon, and although I started on
the journey without speaking of it before I left,
except to my most intimate friends, I know now
by unmistakable proofs that I was watched even
then by unfriendly eyes. It seemed that such
espionage had already gone on for a good while,
as several of my servants afterwards confessed,
when inquiries were made by lawyers, that they
had been led to leave the house at night and
give information to my relations as to everything
passing in my house. Some admitted that they
had been bribed to make false statements about
me, and others told me that they had declined
to act so treacherously. I was obliged to leave

my tiny cottage in the Alps, where I had taken up my abode very early in spring, as the boys could not stand the climate. I had been nursing them continually, especially the young lad, who was seriously ill with fever. Being obliged, therefore, to reach the other side of the Alps, and not wishing to take the long railway road through the Tyrol and Switzerland, I resolved to cross the mountains on foot. I was told that it was the worst part of the year for such an enterprise.

This was, perhaps, the most romantic incident connected with my southern tour. It was early spring, but, with a Tyrolese guide and a devoted Christian boy who had rendered me such stout yeoman service, I risked the ascent. We were unable on account of the deep snow to follow the Stelvio road, and were obliged to cross by a path which had never before been traversed, when covered with snow, by a woman's foot. Thus we unwittingly performed a feat which even the gentlemen of the Alpine Club have been trying in vain to accomplish for the past forty years. On starting, I had no idea that this path would frequently lead us into great danger. Sometimes the snow was almost up to my waist, and I fainted from sheer weariness. But the Lord helped me, and by dint of perseverance we gained the summit, when it occurred to me that, geographically speaking, I occupied the highest position of any woman in Europe. Having started the previous evening by moonlight, we reached the top early on the morning of Easter day.

Never before did I so thoroughly understand why Christ ascended a mountain when He wished to pray in solitude, and never have I had such an Easter day before. The grand quietness of nature in the midst of those white icy giants, undisturbed by any human voice, gave my soul time to rest in exquisite peace and stillness at the foot of God's throne.

A few days later, some English ladies were desirous to speak with me near Como with a view to attempting the task which I had accomplished ; but I said we had taken the route from necessity, and dissuaded them from the rash undertaking. This journey and the sojourn in the Tyrol refreshed me greatly. On my return in the spring I was unable to open my 'Homes' because of the interference of the committee and their refusal to hand over to me any of the funds collected in my name. I had crippled my own resources by advancing over £900 from my private capital, at their suggestion and relying upon their promises. They asked me to accept £150 in final settlement, but I could not conscientiously take it; and I am anxious that it should be distinctly known that I claimed then, and do still claim, the full amount as my just right.

Having now got rid of its best members, the committee became a business concern. Public-houses were established, in connection with which expensive meals were provided; and, to give them a 'Christian' appearance, scripture texts were affixed to the walls, and a 'Christian Brother' dispensed the beer with a 'God bless the draught to you!'

This alarming state of things compelled me to take decisive action. In the first place I was anxious that the fishermen should not think me in any way responsible for the change. I

therefore advertised that my 'Homes' would
be closed for a year, and, to protect my men
from supporting the beer-houses, I announced
that I would recommence my work in the spring.
I knew my fishermen too well to doubt for a
moment that they would rally round me on my
return, how humble soever my 'Homes' might be.

I began to save every farthing for this struggle
against the beer interest and in defence of my
tempted 'children.' Some thirteen sick ladies and
children, who had enjoyed the free air at my villa,
I sent with all reasonable haste away. I closed a
little asylum I had established for children, and
reduced my household expenses to the utmost.
My establishment now included only my foster-
children and two grown-up lads, one of them
suffering still from frequent attacks of fever which
rendered him delirious. Moreover, I had in the
house a dirty little girl whose mother had once
been my servant. This latter was my house-
maid. A governess came daily to teach my
boys and to write for me. I often took my
place in the kitchen, and, despite the fact that
in England, German and Scandinavian ladies are

supposed to be deeply versed in the mysteries of the culinary art, I must confess my ignorance of this very necessary department of household management, and I frankly admit that my cooking experiences were as distasteful to me as the dishes which I tried to mix together.

Thinking that even this I could do for Christ's sake, I did it. Little did I imagine, however, that, in burning my fingers at the kitchen oven, and in slaving at work for which I was not fitted, I was saving money which, instead of going to my fishermen, was to be stolen, thrown away, and given to my gaolers, cruelly to ruin my health, to spoil my life, and almost break my heart. My spirit, however, they could not break. It belongs to Christ, and, because rooted in Him, the storms of trials have only strengthened its growth.

II

THE PLOT

'A man's foes shall be they of his own household.'

MY father was an evangelical Christian; my mother had been a Romanist, and never seemed to understand the new faith which she accepted shortly after her marriage. So long as my father lived I was sure of considerate treatment; when he died I found that thorough and active acceptance of the teaching of Jesus was still able to set mother against daughter, and brother against sister. Then I had made my will in favour of my youngest brother, who was under guardianship, and this gave great offence. Painful as it may seem to mention these matters, yet no alternative is possible. Later events have made them public. Suffice it to say that the breach between my family and myself was completed when I surrendered my heart to

Christ. In my endeavour to obey literally the commands of Jesus, I devoted my life and fortune to Christian work.

After my father's death I was turned out of doors by my family without the slightest reason, unless it was that I meant Christianity to be a reality and not a form, and that I had made the before-mentioned will. Although I was forbidden to return home, and my attempts at reconciliation were badly met, in the eyes of the world it was for appearance · sake represented that I was staying away of my own free will. Now and then letters were even sent to me (and were shown to others), in which I was asked in a kindly tone not to remain obstinately away from home ; but whenever I believed them and went, I was most harshly sent away. In reality every tie was broken years ago, but I thought it my duty to seek reconciliation as long as possible. After being several times asked 'if there were no means to be found to get rid of such an intruding person,' and having been treated in a manner which I had never thought possible in such a sphere of society, I gave up trying and stayed away. It had cost me many tears and much heartbreaking until it came to this; but, as my time and life were wanted for the Lord's work, I resolved to linger no longer at the grave of my earthly love. Christ repaid me fully for it. So I tried to forget, and went on my way. This was made easy for me as no family news ever reached me. I did not even know how many children there were in the families of my brothers and sisters. Still, I had asked in the name of Jesus for all their souls, and stood, and still stand, in the hope of meeting them in eternity. The Lord has many ways of drawing souls to Himself.

Only at long intervals did I accidentally meet with one or another member of the family, and as, on these rare occasions, I was treated very coolly, the conversations were only brief and formal. How great, then, was my joy when, after many years of estrangement, I received an invitation to come and see my family and be reconciled to them! I could not well leave my little home, the boys being delicate and the elder one subject to his attacks; but I immediately went to see the family in response to the invitation. The letter had been written by my youngest brother, and it was the first time I had seen his handwriting, as never in my life had I been the recipient of a letter from him. He proposed to travel with me, and offered as a contribution to my mission work to defray the expenses of the journey. Ah, little did I guess that it was a trap to catch me and to inflict on me an injury much worse than murder! As regards the gift to my mission, I learned later that I had to pay the whole expense of the journey. In my ignorance I was happy, although I felt the immense gulf that had arisen between me and the members of my family, all my views having become so entirely different from theirs under the influence of Christian truth.

After the lapse of some days I received a letter informing me that the patient in my villa was suffering from one of his attacks. I had left him alone in charge of the children, sending the others on a trip home, so that I was obliged to start immediately. This saved me for the time. I understand now the anonymous letters which

warned me not to go into town with members
of my family, and to escape back to Denmark
as quickly as possible.   These communications
referred to rumours of a trap they had laid
for me at Hamburg, and I was afterwards told
that people in the service of my brother had
heard and given the warning. Not a suspicion
arose in me that my relations meant to wrong
me, although I knew that my youngest brother
was discontented at my having changed my will
in favour of my boys and the mission. I even
asked him to accompany me to Kiel, because I
had promised not to travel alone, and because
these warnings were continually reaching me.
Probably I only escaped him that time again
through a boy whom I had sent from my
' Homes ' to become a sailor, and who met me
at the station, and remained with me until after
midnight, when the ship left.

To my astonishment I heard no more of the
members of my family for a long time.   But
the inmates of my house, especially the school-
mistress, received threatening letters 'immediately to leave the Countess, or . . .' At last

the warnings came quite straight, that my relations 'had laid a fiendish trap for me.' My youngest brother would be the one to entrap me, to make me disappear, and have me kept a prisoner for life, which, under the circumstances, would not be long. · I should never leave my house without a man accompanying me. I laughed heartily at this, and said, 'Now I see that the whole story has been invented only to make me afraid. I will just show them that I am not.' Hence I did not observe the promise I had given to my friends, and went to town (Copenhagen) with one of the little boys as my only companion. There I intended to speak to a Christian doctor who had given me advice as to the method of treatment to be observed in the case of my young patient at home if I wished him to get well.

The poor fellow had had some severe attacks, and was out of his senses at the time of my visit to Copenhagen, so that it was difficult for me to keep him, although the Lord had again and again most wonderfully heard my prayers. I have found from repeated experience that prayer is the best medicine; but as others objected to my having employed no physician, I resolved to ask the doctor to take the patient for a while to town and attend to him in his own house. Believing that I was reconciled to the members of the family, I drove at once to my youngest brother's house, asking if I might stay the night, as it was late. To my surprise I was met with a refusal. 'Why, mother, how could you kiss that big man?' asked one of my little boys, whom I had brought with me, and who looked so nice with his long, curly hair, and dressed in his sailor's suit. My explanation puzzled him. 'But, mother, you must not kiss him. He made eyes like what the devil must have. He will do you harm.' Later on, after the mischief had been done, and when my boy was restored to me looking like a broken old man, he said to me, 'Why did you not listen to me? I told you he was a bad man.'—'How did you know it?' I asked.—'Did you not see how he looked at you when we were leaving? and did you not hear him say that he would like to have me whipped and do hard work?'

I was unsuspecting of those around me. The

careful training of the Empress had led to my being kept in ignorance of much of the evil in society. And yet I thank her for it—the world looks better when so seen. I was soon to be rudely awakened from my innocent dreams!

III

THE TRAP

EARLY the following morning, as I sat with my
child in the dining-room of the little hotel, my
brother entered (accompanied by a gentleman).
Never before had I been thus visited by him, and
I rejoiced greatly to see him, thinking that his
coming was in answer to my prayers. Ignorant of
his real intention, and regardless of the warning of
the child, I ran to embrace him, and thought him
actuated by kind feeling when he said to me in
an undertone : 'As I understood you were anxious
to consult a doctor respecting one of your people,
I have brought my friend, Dr. Pontoppidan, who
is willing to go down to your villa in the country
and look at him. Let me also render some little
assistance by bearing the expense and accompanying my friend.'

Hereupon he presented to me a gentleman

K

who looked more like an actor than a doctor, and who asked me to describe the case to him in few words. We were shown to an unoccupied room, where we conversed together for about ten minutes on the case and on absolutely no other topic. I warned him not to believe all that the patient might say, and I mentioned that in his delirium he confused facts with fancies. If the boy should mention the Anarchists he was not to be surprised, as I had engaged in mission work among them. 'How long have you nursed him?' asked Pontoppidan. 'At intervals for nearly one and a half years,' I replied. 'A lady among Anarchists, and alone with delirious patients!' he exclaimed; 'are you not afraid? Are your nerves not affected by it?' and the look of admiring surprise which accompanied his words convinced me afterwards that he was guilty of a crime and not a mere blunder when he testified that I was dangerously insane and under the delusion that I was being persecuted by Anarchists and members of my family. At the time I simply said that I was not by nature timid, but that, on the contrary, I had nerves of iron.

The doctor left, and I returned to my brother in the dining-room. He proposed that his friend and he should go down to my house by the next train, and that I should remain in town to transact my business until they returned to tell me the result of the diagnosis. My brother suggested that they might, if I wished it, remove the patient at once to the People's Hospital. I positively refused, on the ground that I had heard the place had a bad reputation. If it should be necessary to bring the patient to town I could arrange to place him in a private house. My brother mentioned that the hospital would be cheaper. 'I don't care,' I said; 'I will never put any sick person in a place in which I am not fully convinced he will be properly treated. My principle is, that when God sends sickness to my house, He means it to be a cross on me and my house, and I have no right to transfer it to others. It is for me to tend the sick, and pray for them until they recover. So that it would only be for a short time, in any case, that I would allow the boy to be placed under the care of others, to enable me to hold a series of meetings in Sweden, for which I had made arrangements. During that time he should not be confined to a hospital, but should be under the care of people whom I know and trust.'

I was then told that the doctor had sent his carriage to convey my brother to the station ; but I was requested first to drive in it to the doctor's private residence, and there sign a paper authorising my brother to enter my house and examine the patient. This seemed the more necessary as neither of them was known to any of my people. My little boy had in his hand a bag containing important legal papers, several of the warning letters I had received, together with some portions of an Exposition I had written of the Revelation of St. John, which I wished to read to some Christian friends. My travelling-bag, containing sewing materials, purse, letters, brushes, etc., was, when my brother came, somewhere in the dining-room, or in the adjoining steward's office. It was a diminutive bag, and contained, among other curiosities, the tiny revolver to which reference has already been made, and a little bag of white powder which I used for

my face when the weather was cold. These
things were known to my brother from his
childhood, as I had often bidden him in those
days not to play with them.

When I was leaving the hotel to go with my
brother, I looked for this bag, but could not
find it. As it contained my purse and letters,
I requested the attendant to look for it and
have it ready for me on my return. I little
guessed that my brother and the doctor, even
before my conversation with the latter, had pur-
loined it, that they might produce the revolver
and the powder as proofs of a double lie which
they had devised, to the effect that I had
attempted to shoot the doctor, when left alone
with him, and that he had with difficulty pre-
vented me from swallowing a deadly poison.
These were proofs that I was dangerously mad !
Unfortunately for the reputation of their lie, it
was afterwards made clear in evidence that I was
not in possession of the bag during my interview
with the doctor, and that the poison in question
was a perfectly harmless *poudre de riz*, and the
revolver was so rusty that it would not shoot.

In the cab my brother seemed restless, and asked me where I kept my jewels. I told him, and added that as they were not family jewels I intended to dispose of them in behalf of my mission. 'You shall do no such thing,' he said. 'We should like to have them.'—'Yes,' I replied; 'I can easily manage that. I will have them valued, and you can pay me the interest on the amount as long as I live, and you can have the jewels as soon as you like.'—'Oh, no,' he said; 'we would rather you left them with us.'—'But that can't be,' I said. I do not remember whether I then said to him—as I have since said—that for every pearl on my necklace I hoped to bring a soul to heaven, and that such jewels I would keep for ever.

We drove into the court of the People's Hospital; and to my expression of astonished surprise that we had come to such a place, my brother replied that the doctor lived there. The moment we entered the house three men sprang to the door and guarded it. My little boy had been left outside, and I was on the point of going back to fetch him, when one of the men

said, 'You must not open the door, it is not
allowed here.' At this instant the child pushed
his way in, and, clinging to me, said, 'Come,
mother; he will do you some harm. Can't
you see it in his eyes?'—'Nonsense, my boy,'
I said; and, as the air of the place was foul,
I bade him play outside until I came for him.
Poor child, what did he not suffer after this!
I was leaving him in the hands of his enemies.
Under the mask of benevolence he was fearfully
ill-treated.

My brother said, 'It is very difficult to get
anybody into such an establishment without a
doctor's certificate.' Thinking that he spoke of
the sick lad, I whispered to him as he passed me:
'He shall not be brought to this place. It will not
be good for him.' Believing that I was being
taken to the doctor's house, I allowed myself to
be led through two or three courts until we came
to a building somewhat hidden from view. I
was shown the way upstairs to a waiting-room,
where I found a nurse, who on seeing me became deathly pale. 'Are *you* the Countess
Schimmelmann?' she asked. I was afraid she

was about to faint, and said, 'I can see how tired you are. Have you been overworked?'—'Yes,' she answered, and bent her head over some papers on the table. She was the matron of this horrid place, and—a fact which I did not then know—the sister of a cook whom I had sent away in disgrace.

This happened on the 21st of February 1894.

IV

A HUMAN HELL

MY brother left me on the pretext that he would go round for the conveyance, and saying that the doctor would soon be there. After a while a young man came in and said to me with a sneer: 'Now, Countess, you are going to stay here!' I laughed and said: 'You are mistaken, I am waiting for another doctor who requires some directions respecting a patient.' To my surprise he kept on telling me that I was to remain in the hospital.

At first I regarded it as an impertinent practical joke, and told him that I was not accustomed to such liberties from young people. But when a door in the corridor opened and I saw women raving in their madness, tearing their hair and tossing wildly about on their beds, I became alarmed. The young man ordered me to follow him. I refused; but when he took me by my wrist and threatened to use force, I could not but comply, and I went with him, the nurse following us.

I saw at a glance that the doors were well locked, and that escape was impossible; but I was stupefied with amazement, and suffered myself to be led through several corridors, the doors being locked behind us as we passed on. At last we reached a ward of which the accompanying rough sketch may enable the reader to form some approximate idea. The ward was locked at both ends, but all the doors inside the ward were open.

Let it be borne in mind that I did not enter this human hell either voluntarily or on medical certificate; and let me add that the place was practically under no police supervision, nor was visiting allowed.

To resume: the ward was divided into cells, smaller and less comfortable than those of the Berlin prisons. Each cell contained a very rough iron bed; a mattress of sea-weed or straw or some such material, and as hard as wood; a clumsy wooden table so coarsely made that in shape it always reminded me of an elephant; and, in some of the cells, an old dirty chair. The whole

OPEN DOOR

CHAIR

B E D   OPEN DOOR

TABLE

THE SIXTH WARD OF THE PEOPLE'S HOSPITAL

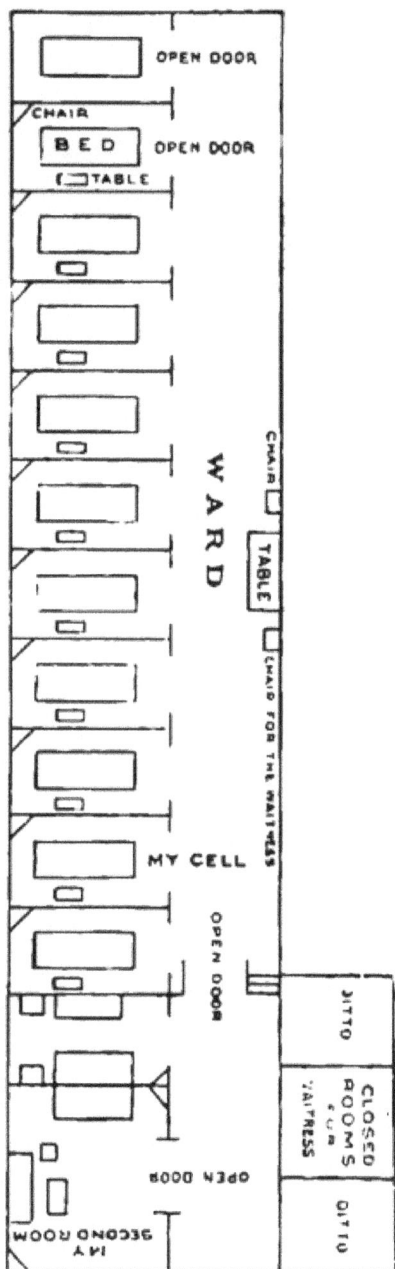

W A R D

CHAIR

TABLE

CHAIR FOR THE WAITRESS

MY CELL

OPEN DOOR

DITTO

CLOSED ROOMS FOR WAITRESS

DITTO

OPEN DOOR

MY SECOND ROOM

cell was not much broader than the doorway, and the door was always kept so wide open that for some time I was under the impression that the cells were without doors. The doors, indeed, were of no use whatever for privacy. It was different with the windows. These were often covered with shutters, and all the light the cell received came through little iron gratings placed in the top of the shutters.

It will, I think, be quite understood that the whole ward was really only one apartment—and what a scene it presented to me when I entered! Passage and cells were alike occupied by scream-ing, shouting, weeping females. Some lay on the beds: one or two seemed to be in a dying condition. Among them there danced a most beautiful young woman in a white night-dress, her long black hair falling around her, and making the marble whiteness of her regular features look startlingly ghostlike.

I gazed on this wild, weird scene as one in a dream; and only awoke to the stern and hor-rible reality of my situation when I was ordered by the young man to take off my clothes. I

indignantly objected, and demanded to be released. I warned them that the crime they were
committing in thus entrapping me could not be
kept secret. He only sneered and laughed, and,
shrugging his shoulders, said : 'Come, now, if you
do not undress yourself, I will do it for you.' He
seized me by the wrist, and was about to carry
his threat into execution, when I said : 'Leave me
this instant and go out of the cell. As I cannot
resist by force, I must comply, and will do it myself.' I then undressed, and was given an old
grimy jacket with a number on the left arm. I
was then ordered to bed, and my garments were
taken away.

Now broke in upon my mind the full truth of
what had happened to me. I remembered the
warnings—they were come true! I remembered
my will, altered in favour of my foster-children,
and the full danger of their position dawned upon
me. The one whom I had brought to town, and
whom, poor child, I had left in the court of the
hospital, waiting for 'mother,' had now fallen help-
lessly into the hands of his enemies, who had not
shrunk from a crime ten times worse than murder

Was it possible that one of my age and experience could, in the nineteenth century, be stolen in broad daylight, and in Copenhagen, where I was so well known? The very audacity of the act had made it possible. For who would dream of seeking me in this place? If by any chance my whereabouts should be discovered, who would believe that my relatives and the doctor had brought me there without cause, and without complying with the laws of the country?

To be looked upon as mad by souls not yet saved, who had received the message of salvation from my lips, and as mad through morphine (for so they gave it out in Berlin) by people whom I had warned against brandy —this was a trial compared with which death would have been welcome! Imprisonment and the degrading treatment following it; the bodily need and privation; the unhealthy confinement (without proper exercise) in bad air, amongst the most defiled of women; as well as the lack of any occupation,[1] I could have borne,—but I

---

[1] Even my Bible was taken from me. Later on I got it, as well as some occupation, through the interference of a nurse.

could *not* bear the thought that so many, many
souls, whom I had told of the love of Christ,
and of the wonders He is able to perform to-day
as well as in ancient times, especially as on
one occasion I had been told that these souls
should be my testimony;—no, I could not
endure the thought that the devil should be
allowed to mar the work which God had begun
through me in the souls of so many—to see it
ruined through their being told that the testimony had been that of a madwoman, or, worse
still—as it was put—that I had become mad
through the use of morphine. What a hypocrite
they would believe me to be, if they now heard
that I, who had been working for years to show
them the sin of getting drunk on brandy, had
myself practised the same vice in another form
—I who had openly refused for years to take
medicine, because I had accepted Christ as my
Healer! I had laid my hands on the sick
when my Master had sent me, and always
found that, if He gave me the command to do
it, He was mighty enough to heal.

Strong as were my nerves and my mind with

the strength which Christ had given me, I believed it absolutely impossible for any one in his right mind to regard me as insane in any other sense than that in which some people profess to treat Christianity itself as a form of insanity. Oh, how hideous a crime it was to stop my work in this way! Had they only had the courage to murder me, how much fairer that would have been! Gladly had I changed my lot to this, so as not to bring doubt into minds struggling towards the light! Such were my thoughts at that dreadful moment; but the next thing that occurred to me was: 'It *is* a form of martyrdom, and will some day yield fruit.' I resolved to stand firmly against any temptation to lower the standard of my faith. I knew that to pray *aloud* would be about the worst thing I could do to recommend my case, but just on that account I did it. I remember falling on my knees, and praying with bitter tears: 'O God, no one *can* do anything which Thou dost not permit; and if Satan is now attempting to silence in this prison the lips which have testified of Jesus, let even this tend to the furtherance and welfare of Thy

Kingdom. Grant me in this hour my prayer
that this attempt of the evil one to close my lips
may be frustrated, and that through me, as a
humble instrument, Thy gospel may yet be
carried to thousands.' In my desperation I used
great words, and added: 'Unto distant lands
over half the world, and even to the far away
islands of the sea.' I state this to the glory of
God, because it has become true.

Mocking faces and rude remarks brought back
my thoughts to earth. Where was I? I was at
a loss fully to understand. Lunatics of the worst
description surrounded me; but it was not until
later that I ascertained that the place in which I
was immured was a station to which the police
brought men and women who had become mad
in prison, or who simulated insanity as an excuse
for their crimes. Cases of *delirium tremens*, of
those driven by madness to commit murder, and
of half-dead, would-be suicides, were lodged here
until they could be otherwise disposed of.

It was the depth of winter, and the Danish
cold was piercing; yet when they took my own
woollen clothes away, the nurse brought me only a

little greyish cotton jacket with a number stamped on one of the arms.[1]   They compelled me to use that dreadful bed, hard and cold, its two little woollen covers all stained.   A whim in which I had always indulged was to take my own bed-clothes with me wherever I went—even to Court or to an hotel.   I had everything with me, as well as ample linen and clothes for some weeks; but, although the trunk was there,[2] they neverthe-less kept its contents from me.   In regard to my own garments, I need only briefly say that after my sojourn of nearly six weeks in that horrid place, I was in such a ragged and filthy condition that on my entering the state asylum one of the nurses lent me some of her own linen, and the doctor, out of his own purse, bought me several articles indispensable to my toilet.   No one who has not passed through some similar experience can imagine the pain of such close contact with uncleanness, or the sense of relief it is to get into

[1] Later on I received a woollen jacket.
[2] The trunk stood in the ward.   My brother had it brought from the hotel in my name, in order that the people there should not get alarmed, finding that I did not return; then it was brought to the hospital, and disappeared with me behind the walls of the ward.

L

the neighbourhood of baths and clean clothes again.

The restless and howling inmates were continually passing my open door, and even came into my cell and tried to creep under the bed. I did not mind them; but when I thought of the cruelty of those who, under pretence of affection, had decoyed me to this place of shame, I wept, and could not cease to weep, and did not before know that my poor old eyes were capable of so many tears. Such cruelty was a mystery to me. In all my dealings with criminals and drunkards in my mission work (and I had met the very worst of these), I had never encountered one who dared to do me harm, and I remembered one of them saying, when a companion suggested that I was running a great risk in going among such men : ' The man is not to be found who could be bad enough to injure her.' Yet it had been done, and by whom? When they told me that I was a prisoner—and far worse than a mere prisoner—by order of my family, I called them liars! Reflection on the part my brother had played in the tragedy convinced me, however, that it must be true.

I tried to explain my position to the attendants
—they heeded me not. I spoke to a nurse respecting the poor child left outside in the court,
and asked that he might be taken care of—she
treated my request with indifference. Indifference, however, soon changed to insult. The
first to offend was a young doctor, who treated
me with insulting indignity, although I was too
sorry to take much notice of it. I told four
students who were passing through the ward
that I was a Countess and perfectly sane; and
was laughed at for my pains! All the students
did not treat me in this way: there were some
gentlemen among them. One of them, in the
hearing of the doctors, asked what proofs had
been adduced of my insanity; and when he was
told the story of the revolver and the powder, he
laughed in their faces and said, 'Childish nonsense! It is absurd to declare a woman mad on
such evidence! There is not the slightest trace
of mental aberration!'

Another student whispered to me, 'You will
soon be released, Countess; only remain quiet and
natural as you are now. We have a press and a

public opinion.' Meanwhile my durance was vile indeed. I can only give specimens of the treatment meted out to me. Despite the hard bed and the cold, I slept soundly. I was nevertheless ordered to take morphine in large quantities, and it was only my absolute refusal to touch it, and the pity of the nurse, that saved me from the dangerous drug. The nurses were constantly about me. I enjoyed no privacy. They reported all I said and did, and told me things I shuddered to hear. On one occasion they related to me the story of a murderess who had been there, but was found to be perfectly sane. The woman had barbarously murdered a little boy in the Asylum, and was now sentenced to death.[1] The story was so revolting that I had refused to read the details of it in the papers at the time, and then they suggested that I should use the bath which she had been the last to use before she was taken away to be sentenced to death. After some days I was removed to a larger apartment, at the end of the ward, which had been occupied by six delirious drunkards, who

[1] Möller.

were now removed. My cell was then allotted
to a murderess,[1] and her successor was a girl of
the streets who died of disease and in child-bed
shortly after she came in. I draw a veil over
the revolting details of the case, and of the post-
mortem examination which took place in the cell
within a few hours after her death.

I am not recording the most terrible of my
experiences in that den of sorrow and infamy.
These I have related to the Danish Minister of
Police, and may, if occasion requires, make them
public later on.

One suit of my clothes was restored to me,[2]
and I made a point of getting all the exercise
I could by walking up and down in the ward,
although the bad air of the ill-ventilated and
sometimes fully occupied ward neutralised my
efforts. Instead of a daily bath, I had to wash
myself in a tiny basin. This was seldom to be
done properly for fear of being in full view of

[1] A suicide who had taken poison, and died in an awful manner
there in the ward.

[2] Later I got also a woollen jacket with a number on the arm.
Two nurses insisted on getting me a new one from their stores in
the hospital, but they had to fight hard before obtaining it.

male attendants and assistants, who had free
access at all times to the ward. One day I locked
my door, and asked the nurse to stand before it
until I washed. Immediately Pontoppidan came
himself. The nurse asked him to pass, as I
was washing ; but he threw open the door, with
a sneering remark. I suffered intensely from
thirst, as I was unable to drink out of the glass
used by the women, whose faces were covered
with eczema, and the water in the ward was bad.
I asked for soda-water, but it was a long time
before my request was acceded to, and even
then they gave me only a dozen small bottles
during the whole period of my stay. They told
me it was too expensive! I often wept from
thirst. Touching the matter of expense, let me
here interpolate the remark that Pontoppidan
received out of my estate, which nobody had a
right to touch, five hundred crowns for making
his false attestation, and about ten shillings
per day (for my board and lodging), etc. etc.,
although, as a matter of fact, Pontoppidan had
no claim to remuneration of any kind. He was a
salaried official, and the other physicians whom

I afterwards met in the state asylums take nothing, and they even decline little presents in token of remembrance lest it should have the appearance of bribery.

My breakfast consisted of one or two cups of bad tea and a few slices of bread, covered with something which should have been butter. No knife was allowed me; and I have seen a nurse feeding a madwoman covered with eczema, by forcing every bit with her finger into her throat, turn from her revolting task to prepare my bread and butter. If I did not eat, my nerves would be shattered; if I overcame my disgust and partook of the food, I might catch the infection of some foul disease.

Only God Himself knows what prayer and effort it cost me to overcome my disgust, and to see it to be my duty to eat the nauseous food, and thus escape the greater of the dangers that threatened me, and keep my nerves intact. These I was determined should not be allowed to break down or even weaken.

My midday meal consisted of a watery gruel, with a little bad fish or bread and meat. Having taken my resolution, I did not pay much attention to the food.

A girl belonging to the Salvation Army had earlier been brought in. She had fainted in the street, and had fallen into the clutches of the doctor. During her detention, from which after a few days she was rescued through the intervention of the Army, she assured me that, although they were not accustomed in the cadet schools of the Army to scrutinise their food very closely, she was quite unable to swallow the articles of diet provided in the hospital. In the evening two cups of tea and three thin slices of bread and butter were supplied to me. One of the nurses, who was indignant at my treatment, asked for a little cold meat for me. After long negotiations the request was acceded to, and I received each evening, in gracious concession, *one* very tiny anchovy!

Quite suddenly, however, this method of treatment was changed. Instead of spare diet, I was allowed a substantial beefsteak at noon, and at five o'clock the luxury of a cup of coffee. The secret of this unexpected reversal of policy I could not guess. So strangely terrible, however, is the fact I am about to relate, that I might hesitate to place it on record were I not able to prove its accuracy by adducing the certificate of those who witnessed it.

I was well aware that the doctor and several of his nurses were perpetually on the look-out for something in my deportment which they could construe into a proof of my insanity. They watched me also at meal-times, and, if ever I looked closely at anything on my plate, they asked me if I was afraid of poisoning. I therefore made it a practice to keep my eyes on the ceiling or on the walls while eating the large pieces of meat which, as I was without a knife, were cut for me. One day I perceived something hard in the meat, but, thinking that it was some small pieces of bone, I swallowed them without remark. When it occurred again, however, I looked carefully at my beefsteak, and found small iron nails in it. They were without heads, and were placed within the steak perpendicularly, so that when it was cut they could not be seen. I called the nurse and showed her the meat and the nails, and she, in turn, very indignantly showed them to some medical students who were passing at the time. Later on I obtained the certificate of an eyewitness in attestation of the fact, as I was anxious that people should not declare me insane when I told them that I still suffered from the presence in my body of shoemaker's nails, for such they proved to be! Poisoning by ground-glass is known to the world; but who ever before heard of poisoning by shoemaker's nails?

Pontoppidan came and asked me whether I regarded the occurrence as due to malice or to accident, and I was obliged to answer guardedly. If I had said by malice, he would have used my reply to bolster up his lying theory of mental derangement; and as I was unwilling to remove from the hospital the stigma of what had taken place, I told him that the nails were swallowed, and that the effects would not be in the least degree affected by my description of the cause as accidental or malicious. I still leave it an open question as to how the presence of nails in the beefsteak is to be accounted for.

Towards the end of my stay in the place, I was allowed the privilege, invariably extended in other prisons to the worst of criminals, of taking exercise in a little courtyard surrounded with high walls; and from the windows of Pontoppidan's private apartments, which commanded a view of my promenade, I was sometimes watched by men and women, whose faces, however, I was unable to distinguish. I resolved that my jailors should not see me weep, and I gave them no opportunity of triumph. By-and-by the nurse found it too tiresome to climb the steps, so, opening a door, she led me round and round the house. There was no fresh air, and the sense of captivity was dreadful; but the recreation was a relief to my feet, which had grown stiff from lack of exercise. *Pontoppidan saw this, flew into a rage, and put a stop to it!*

Painful as was this physical bondage, it was the lightest chain I had to carry. The mental and moral fetters which my tormentors forged for me were infinitely more galling. It has ever since been to me a subject of thoughtful wonder how God protected my frail life and sustained

my fainting heart during those days of darkness.
To one who had been so carefully shielded from
the evils of society, and who was so innocent
of the depths of depravity in human nature, the
terrible things which my raving companions in
that dreadful den *said and did* seemed to present
to me a picture of hell itself. Of such things
I had never had the faintest idea. I breathed
the atmosphere of a moral miasma. Every feeling of my nature was outraged. Without entering
at present into particulars, I may add that if the
doctor, whose duty it was to guard his fellow-
beings against unnecessary injury of body and
agony of mind—even in that place of shame—
had been actuated by common human sentiments,
my lot would have been, if not tolerable, yet less
outrageously cruel ; but it became a living martyrdom through the co-operation of Mr. Pontoppidan
with the sane and the insane to disturb my
mental balance and to fill me with the appre-
hension of evils of the very worst description.

Before passing on to speak of my deliverance,
I will mention the most despicable—though perhaps not the cleverest—device invented by my

enemies for their own protection. Mr. Pontoppidan came and informed me that my foster-children had been placed in the hands of a laundress who hated me because I had refused to give her alms on account of her manner of life. Before I was entrapped I had been told that they should be 'ruined in body and soul'; and as my imprisonment, which had also been threatened, was now a realised fact, my concern for the fate of the boys can be imagined. What they passed through was very hard. Every means was used to injure and deprave them, but their innocence was graciously preserved to them, doubtless by means of their natural simplicity, which they have only slowly outgrown. Many obstacles had to be surmounted before I succeeded in regaining possession of them on my release. They were given up to me bearing cruel marks of the violence with which they had been used, and looking like thoroughly broken old men. Willie's first prayer on his return was: 'O Jesus, it has been a hard fight, but Thou hast given us the victory. Let us not have another fight like that. Let us rather die.'

Later on, when it became apparent that I was
not to be robbed of my reason, and when the
results of this infamous plot had aroused the
fears of my persecutors, it was proposed that
if I would promise to say that I had entered
the hospital of my own free will and in search
of rest, or that I had been insane, and if I would
further promise that I would not continue my
mission work, the children would be immediately
restored to me! If not, vengeance would be
taken on them. The thought of the heroic
mother of the Maccabees came to my help.
Could she sacrifice her seven sons to avoid the
forbidden meat, and could I not entrust these
children, whom I only took for Christ's sake,
to the mercy of God? The children had
become very dear to me, and yet, even if they
were to suffer for it, I would never be induced
to tell so black a lie as that I had voluntarily
placed myself in Pontoppidan's power, or that
I had either sought or found rest among the
poor restless souls with whom he compelled me
to associate, or that anything but locks and
bars had kept me for a single hour in an abode

so dreadful. I gave this answer, and as to my
mission work I said that, should I ever escape
from the trap alive, I would, God helping me, do
thrice as much as I had done before. The issue
has justified my resolve. God helped me, and I
am now doing three times more work than before.
God has widened my sphere of work by the very
means by which men tried to limit or destroy
it, and the children are not the less dear to me
for what they have so bravely endured.

V

DELIVERANCE

HAD I been allowed to communicate with my friends it would not have been possible to deprive me of my liberty for as much as two days. But by the refusal of Pontoppidan to allow me any communication, the term of my sufferings extended to five weeks, which seemed to me, encircled with horror as I was, like so many weary years. There were many in high positions who would have interfered had they known of my whereabouts, and many who would have made inquiries had they not been deceived by the report that I had left the country. When rumours of my imprisonment in such a place began to be circulated, some were doubtless deterred from taking active measures for my rescue by false descriptions of my condition and by the lie which they had circulated that I had sought the help of Pontoppidan of my own accord, because my nerves had been shattered by morphine; and that I had the best lodgings and nursing possible.

Kept under so close a surveillance, and deprived of writing materials, I was unable either to write a letter or to get one passed out. Having gained possession of a pencil, however, and finding a small slip of paper, I succeeded in writing a brief note under my bedclothes. An old woman who was being sent home consented to take it with her, but, unfortunately for my stratagem, the nurse caught me in the act of passing it to her. The old woman, to protect herself, professed great surprise that I should think of getting her to do so questionable a deed, but, when the nurse's back was turned, she seized the note and slipped it into her stocking. The attempt was a fruitless one, however. She was found out on leaving the establishment, and my little missive did not reach its destination.

In course of time the rumour that I had gone on a voyage to England or Germany was suspected by my friends to be a ruse to conceal

M

some foul play on the part of my enemies, and
they were unable to credit the story that I was
taking rest with friends. Their suspicions were
also aroused by the manner in which my estate
was being despoiled by those who, on the ground
of my alleged insanity, had had themselves appointed my guardians. To the manner in which
the responsibilities of guardianship were dis-
charged I will refer in my next chapter.

At length a Member of Parliament interviewed
Pontoppidan, and, in his own name and in the
behalf of others, asked him if it were true
that I was lodged in the sixth ward of the
hospital. Pontoppidan could not deny that I was,
but he affirmed that I was so hopelessly mad
that he could not possibly allow any one to ap-
proach me. He was then told that nevertheless
in two days the Member of Parliament would
return and make an effort to see me. Pontoppidan tried to compel me to write a note to the
effect that I declined to see any one. I told him
he would never induce me to tell such a lie.
Being then reminded of the fact that, if his
statement as to my mental condition were really

true, his establishment was not in any respect
a suitable place of habitation for me, and that
according to the law he must have me transferred to a state asylum, he thought it safest
to get me off his hands before the Member
of Parliament reappeared and further inquiries
were made. Of these negotiations I was kept in
ignorance, and Pontoppidan took advantage of my
ignorance to attempt his last, his master-stroke of
inhuman diplomacy, and bereave me of my reason
by robbing me of all hope of release. He broke
in upon me and abruptly told me that it had
been decided to remove me to another asylum,
from which I knew there could be no possible
escape so long as the false certificate of my
supposed madness was not annulled. I gave up
hope for this life at that moment, not knowing
that I was to be transferred to a well-regulated
state asylum and to the care of one of the greatest authorities in mental diseases.[1] Growing pale
and on the point of fainting, somehow I drew

[1] To be 'Overlaege' of 'Ohringe' is the highest position a
medical man can attain in Denmark, and only one at a time
can be appointed to this post.

myself up to my full height, and, stretching my hand towards heaven, I said : 'God is the Judge between us two, doctor ; think of it when the hour of vengeance comes! As for me, you are helping me to win the reward of martyrs.' For one moment I saw the future crown and the victory so clearly, but when left alone it grew dark for me.

Still, I did not despair. The unfailing grace of Christ, which had given me the power to minister to the needs of the wretched and speak words of consolation to the poor and the afflicted, sustained me still, and would sustain! Later one of the alleviations of my sad lot came to me in the form of the simple yet beautiful English hymn :

> 'Art thou weary, art thou languid,
>   Art thou sore distrest?
> "Come to Me," saith One, "and coming,
>   Be at rest."'

It had been suggested to me by a friend shortly before my release, and became the solace of many a sad hour. Especially did I feel that I could derive comfort from the words :

'Finding, following, weeping, struggling,
    Is He sure to bless?
Saints, apostles, prophets, martyrs,
        Answer, Yes!'

In the infirmary, to which I was taken on the
28th March 1894, I received kind treatment. The
authorities were capable and courteous, and, had
I been a fit subject for a lunatic asylum, I might
have been content; but, as it was, the time
passed very wearily and the life was intolerably
tedious, as my heart was full of anxious fear in
regard to the children, my work, and my Homes.
According to our Danish law a certain time
must elapse, during which the state of a patient
is closely observed, before the doctors are allowed
to declare to be false the certificate of insanity
on which any one is admitted. Pontoppidan had
based his certificate on 'distrust of her loving
family, and trust in unworthy people' (perhaps
my poor 'boys'), 'her possession of a revolver
and some white powder, and of a manuscript
of some notes on those portions of the Revelation of St. John which refer to antichrist.'[1]

[1] These notes on the antichrist contained for the most part
only Bible texts from the Prophets and the Revelation of St. John,

He tried to convey the idea that these references to antichrist were superstitions dictated by a mad fear of Anarchism! When I say that in my father's time I was very fond of sport, and that my sisters and I were accustomed to carry and use firearms, and when I again declare that I was, as the events show, alas, only too trustful of my relatives, it will be seen on how slight a foundation the charge was based. In fact, it is rather an acknowledgment of very good behaviour on my part that nothing else could be found in the whole course of my life to serve as a pretext for such a charge. To save himself, Pontoppidan afterwards publicly declared that for several years he had been watching for an occasion to catch me (without ever having seen me), my family having asked him to do so. He produced letters to this effect, which it was professed had been written by my mother, in-

which I had linked together with shortened remarks for my own use. Curiously enough, these Bible texts seemed to be unknown to most of the doctors, and caused even a moment's disturbance in the state asylum, until one of the doctors laughingly produced them, remarking that every Christian held these words holy, and he, too, believed in them.

forming him that I had been mad for many years. Yes, that from my early childhood I had been mad was declared by the members of my family to those who had not known me at that period; while, to those who had known me from my childhood and through the rest of my life, it was said that I had recently become insane— by use of morphine or through influenza. As to the letters, I suppose them to have been forged, as I have sufficient proof that letters of my mother have been forged, even after her death, which occurred about four years before this plot was carried out.

Fortunately, I was now in the hands of our cleverest specialists in mental disease, and they soon declared that they could find in me no trace whatever of mental aberration. In spite of this, my family demanded that, by right of the guardianship they had obtained, I should be handed over to them. They intended, they said, to take me to a surgeon that I might undergo an operation, although the doctors declared there was not the slightest necessity for such a course, the supposed ailment not existing.

They were evidently bent on having me con-
signed to a German asylum. They even sent
two repulsive-looking persons, a man and a
woman, to carry me off by force. At this, the
superintendent was highly indignant, and said
that he would never give me up to the family.
I was free to go where I chose, but he would
advise me to remain as a guest in the asylum
until he had reported the whole affair to the
Minister of Justice. If I left at once, he was
afraid I would be in danger of their violence.
The usual forms were observed, and the guardianship was quickly cancelled.

Meanwhile I took refuge in the castle of
the Grand Duchess Dowager of ——, as the
members of the family were still making
desperate efforts to regain possession of me.
My bodily strength was broken down, and my
restoration to it was very gradual. I shall never
regain the youthful elasticity my wholesome
and active life had helped me to keep. The
treatment to which I was subjected has left an
affection of the heart, which I am afraid will
never leave me.

From my friendly shelter I returned to Denmark, where, from the Royal Family to the little boys in the street, I was received with unbounded kindness and sympathy. A notable personage sent me the message: 'You have all the sympathy and the right of our country on your side—come back to us.' So it was, and this is gratifying, but I prize it only to the extent to which it enables me to fulfil the mission of my life—to bring souls to Christ.

What steps have I taken to bring the authors of my sufferings to justice? None. In Denmark the law does not prosecute an offender except at the instigation of the person wronged. This I have not done as yet, leaving it to God to deal with those who committed the crime. May He bring them to repentance in His own time, by mercy or by judgment! I am compelled, however, to give a statement of these events myself, as I am anxious that they should not appear exaggerated or wrongly represented, but in strict accordance with the facts. In the interests of my work, I place on record this simple statement of the utter failure of a base attempt to ruin my work by first calling in question, and then trying to deprive me of, my reason. I reserve to myself the right to enter more minutely into the experiences through which I passed in the People's Hospital, and to take any steps which subsequent events may render necessary for safeguarding. To very many of those who have heard me, my name is closely associated with their belief in Christ ; and it is for the sake of these, to prevent the doubts which might only too easily arise from false reports, that I especially deem it my duty to state the events of my life as they are. Christ is my Saviour—and He saves from sorrow and sin, and gives health and life. I have *always* experienced this.

MISSION WORK

MISSION WORK

THE day after my imprisonment my brother, against every law, took possession of my property. A guardian was first installed four weeks later in the further course of the intrigue. As the youths were in charge of my house, these would have been its lawful guardians up to that point. That my escape was contrary to the expectation of him and my later 'guardian' was apparent from the state of ruin to which, in my absence, he had wilfully reduced my belongings. An alternative hypothesis is possible. Fearing the worst, they would appropriate or dissipate my little property, so that, in the event of my reappearance, I should find myself deprived of the means of appearing in society or of resuming my mission work, so that the crime done to me might more easily be hidden. His faith in his friend's power to

unhinge my reason,[1] and to keep me for ever out
of his way, was too implicit, however, to permit
of his giving the idea of my release a place in
his humane programme, or of his allowing the
thought of it to interfere with his disposal of my
effects.

His first step was to get rid of the other
members of my household. My foster-children
he had disposed of, and he quietly devised a
method of dislodging the two young lads who
still remained in my house. No sooner was I
placed in safe keeping than Pontoppidan and my
brother entered my villa and took possession.
Amid peals of laughter Pontoppidan made merry
over my letters, and then seated himself at the
harmonium and tried to play. He did not even
speak a word about the health of the patient nor
feel his pulse, but declared him to be perfectly
well. It is certain that, had he looked through
the papers contained in the bag which he had
previously stolen, he must have found, in the
form of several doctors' certificates, ample evidence of the youth's serious condition of health.

[1] Mr. Pontoppidan believed himself to be a great hypnotist.

These certificates had been obtained in proof of
his unfitness for service in the army.

My brother then commanded the lad to deliver
up to him a diamond star worth 25,000 crowns
(he knew well that I had never possessed such
a thing); and since this was not forthcoming, he
called a policeman, gave him a gratuity of 200
crowns, and, denouncing the lads as thieves, had
them taken to the frontier, where they were
presented with a passport to Berlin and sent
away. The invalid I afterwards found, but his
companion, so far as I have been able to discover,
died for want of food on the road.

My brother and his accomplices dismissed
my governess and my servant, and then wreaked
their vengeance on the furniture and all the
effects and appurtenances of the house in which
they were left in sole possession.[1] They burned
my papers, damaged my furniture, and packed
my court-dresses among the utensils of the

[1] A 'guardianship' could only be established after several
weeks—as long as the two youths whom I left in charge of my
house were its lawful keepers. But my brother dislodged them
by force, falling upon them with seven men and a dog, and
usurped the right of possession.

kitchen. My beautiful pony, our pet, they gave to a woman to whom for good reasons I had refused money, and whom I had forbidden to come to the house. My carriage, the last gift I had received from my father, they gave to a drunken workman. Now at length my jewels were 'in the keeping of the family,' although these I afterwards with difficulty succeeded in recovering. The house itself was on the point of being sold at a ruinous price when the so-called 'guardianship' was cancelled. Even my poor cat, which had been given to me in Italy, was hurled into the courtyard with such violence that her leg was broken, and an end was mercifully put to her sufferings by a friendly hand. The damage done to my estate was estimated at 21,000 crowns. The house, when I again entered it, presented a scene of wild confusion.

While this was going on, and I was being robbed of the resources by means of which I had hoped to recommence my mission, my mission property itself was being destroyed. One of the 'Homes' had earlier been burned, and the other was broken up and in part demolished. My little vessel had been left on the beach to be spoilt by the sun.[1] Nothing was left to me but the ruins of my estate and a small capital. My 'guardian' had even tampered with this, and had disposed of a portion of it to defray the expenses of his journeys, etc.

It was at this crisis that, in September 1894, I returned to Denmark and, as I have said, received so cordial a reception from all classes of society. Into a description of the popularity which overtook me I do not wish to enter. To its influence on my extended usefulness in God's service, however, I am obliged to refer.

The whole press with one voice, Conservative and Socialistic alike, took up my cause. An indignant Parliament interfered. The cause of the day was put aside, and in the name of all the different parties the Minister of Justice was informed of the facts and urged to take immediate steps for

[1] Several gentlemen warned the 'guardian' that the ship would be ruined by leaving her on the shore, but he expressly refused to have her put into water. Though she was quite new and had cost me much money (I had carefully saved it to build her), she was returned to me in an utterly ruined state after the 'guardian' was compelled to do so by the lawyers.

N

a reform in the law affecting the questions involved in my imprisonment, and, in particular,
control over the infirmaries.[1] These were speedily
made reformative. The work is not yet completed,
but we are trusting to see the law on this vital
subject placed in a satisfactory state. I now know
that I was not Pontoppidan's only victim. Others
as sane as myself he tried to deprive of their
liberty, and nervous women became almost mad
in his hands. The story of the beautiful young
woman with the long dark hair and marble features, if told as it was told to me by her poor
broken-hearted husband at the close of one of my
meetings, would harrow the feelings of the most
callous. The stories of the clever old Etatsroth
Brunn and of the poor dressmaker girl are only
too well known. In Denmark, in Germany, and
perchance in England, how many there are who,
with nerves less strong and with faith less clear,
have succumbed to their terrible lot, I cannot say ;
but it was in behalf of these that I made up my
mind that if ever I escaped I would allow no

---

[1] It is said that there never was such unity through the whole
Danish press as in my behalf.

personal considerations to deter me from making my case known as a flagrant example of the possibility of perpetrating the most cruel crimes under the pretence of benevolent kindness. I could relate scenes from my own 'drama' that would make the most unfeeling shudder. How easy it must be to deal more effectually with victims of a lower rank in society than myself! That such is the case is proved by the number of appeals I have since received to interfere for the deliverance of persons equally sane, and by the revelations which the discussion of my treatment has called forth. No law, I dare say, will absolutely prevent the evil, but I shall ever regard it as my solemn duty to impress the public with the heinousness of this crime, this worse than murder of innocent men and women in mind and body. This will at least tend to decrease the number of such victims, and it is to help them and to protect an unwary public from a fate so terrible, that I am now giving to the world a brief recital of my experiences.

This, however, will form only an incidental and occasional part of my work. During the past year I have conducted evangelistic meetings in all circles of society. My public meetings have frequently been attended by as many as three thousand persons. These meetings have been richly blessed to many, and I could never have believed it possible that the prayer I offered during the first hour of my imprisonment would be so signally answered. To re-erect my Fishermen's Homes in the Baltic is my chief aim ; and it is my purpose to spend the spring and summer of each year with these seafaring children of mine, among whom I spent my first happy years of Christian service, and who were never absent from my thoughts during the term of my captivity. Meetings for Socialists and workmen, tavern-keepers and street-boys, and any to whom I can bring the glad tidings of salvation, I conduct in all the cities and towns which I visit.

This plan was made possible to me by friends in Denmark. Unable to answer all the calls that came to me or to endure the strain of continual travelling, the idea of a yacht was suggested, by means of which I might resume my work in the Baltic, and undertake, during the winter months, an International Sailors' Mission in places where it was greatly needed. I have enough means left for my own personal requirements, and even to start, and contribute to, this mission ; but it is impossible for me to carry it further on alone on my own account. I am disposing of my estate, my jewels, and indeed all my possessions, to enable me to carry on my work in the Baltic and in the chief ports on both sides of the German Ocean. The yacht *Duen* is the result, and my little cabin is now my only home.

Recently I conducted a mission in Hamburg. Here the sailors of all nations took a deep interest in my work. At a large meeting of Socialists I was greeted with the cry : 'We are not Socialists ; we are Anarchists!' One of their ringleaders stood beside me during my address, flourishing an iron rod close to my face ; but I have no fear, and my offending friend was one of the first to find his way to me after the meeting to speak to me on religion. They are very much the same sort of men as those among whom I had laboured in Berlin. They are atheists to a man, and not a little rough. So much so, indeed, that some Christian gentlemen who accompanied me were alarmed. When I mentioned the 'Blood of Jesus,' they uttered a loud cry of opposition, and some fifty of them rushed from the room, only, however, as my captain told me, to return by another door. My meetings in the largest dancing-saloons and music-halls in Hamburg were crowded to excess by eager and attentive listeners ; and I did not leave the city before I had lifted up my voice against the rationalism of its clergy, which, fifty years ago, the late famous Dr. John Cairns said, 'is here in all its putrescence, or rather skeleton nakedness,'[1] and which is still so largely accountable for the evils which prevail.

At Great Yarmouth, where, a few weeks ago, I took shelter from a storm, I was very soon on the best of terms with the fishermen, among whom, through the kindness of the clergy of the Established and other Churches, I was able to hold a few meetings.

[1] *Life and Letters of John Cairns, D.D., LL.D.* By A. R. MacEwen, D.D. London : Hodder and Stoughton.

It will interest my readers to know that my yacht the *Duen* previously belonged to Prince Waldemar of Denmark, the youngest brother of her Royal Highness the Princess of Wales. I received it in exchange for a little racing cutter. The Queen of Denmark was graciously pleased to suggest a yearly gift to my mission, and accompanied it with an expression of warm interest in my work and earnest wishes for its success. On the arrival of the yacht *Duen* in England, her Royal Highness the Princess of Wales most graciously expressed similar wishes, accompanied by a donation to the mission, in which also several other royal personages of other countries are interested. Friends in Denmark and Germany have followed her Majesty's example; but I am still greatly in need of funds to enable me to carry on my mission:

(1) To the fishermen of the Baltic.

(2) To sailors of all nations in European ports; and

(3) To the distressed and troubled elements of society everywhere.

I keep a large supply of literature in various languages, and the captain and mate of my yacht are devoted Christians, and take an active part in my work. I am a member of the Lutheran Church, but my attitude to Christians of all denominations is briefly expressed by St. Paul: 'Grace be to all them that love the Lord Jesus Christ in sincerity!' The dangers which threaten our common European civilisation, and the evils which in these days imperil the very existence of the Church of Christ, convince me that only in international friendliness and brotherly love is safety to be found.

I appeal to my English fellow-Christians to assist me in my threefold mission. Their generosity, as all the world knows, is not lavished upon their own insular needs, but overflows the great continents of the earth, and does not pass by even the smaller 'islands of the sea.' In the islands of the Baltic, where the neglected fishermen await the return of their 'mother,' I require help from English friends of the Temperance cause to enable me to rebuild, on distinctively Temperance principles, the only 'Homes' for

which my rough 'sons' ever cared. They often
send me word that they are longing not only for
me, but for the warm cup of coffee, and, most of
all, for the gracious message of the gospel which
they say they understand better as explained by
their 'mother' than from anybody else. My
English friends who know anything of my International Sailors' Mission take a special interest
in the efforts I am able to make for the welfare
and protection of their own sailors in foreign
ports, as for instance in Copenhagen, where I hold
meetings for them whenever opportunity offers.[1]

To my English sisters I would say in con-
clusion that the success of women's work on
the Continent depends largely on the success of
the mission which God has entrusted to me.
My narrative has revealed to them afresh the
difficult conditions under which the few women
who, along with myself, are seeking to imitate
their example, and to serve Christ in directions
possible only to our sex, have begun the work
which has attained such large proportions in

[1] In two months I distributed 700 English books and tracts
and New Testaments.

England and America. We working women on the Continent have a hard battle to fight. If I triumph over the obstacles which still beset me, many others will be encouraged to give themselves to the same, or to similar, work. If, after having sacrificed everything to follow in the footsteps of Christ, I am obliged to retire from the field, those who have the courage to attempt to go similar ways will doubtless have to contend against more inveterate prejudices and to pass through still greater tribulations.

The aim of my life is to do the will of our common Master by ministering to the needs of the tempted, the oppressed, and the suffering brethren 'for whom Christ died.' Joyfully do I place at the feet of Jesus everything which the world counts dear. Wealth, rank, titles, honours, friends, comfort, and even reputation, I gladly resign. In surrendering body and soul freely to Christ, a joy is to be found which brings present recompense for the bitterest sufferings it involves : a joy so glorious that in its radiance the pleasures of earth fade to nothingness, a joy which is to be found only in the love of Christ.

APPENDIX

APPENDIX

Extract from Parliamentary Report, October 16, 1894

THE CASE OF THE COUNTESS SCHIMMELMANN

Speech by Mr. G. Jensen, Member for Belum

'THE subject on which I wish to speak is one of the greatest interest to the whole country, concerning as it does the incarceration of the Countess Adeline Schimmelmann in the Sixth Ward of the People's Hospital. I have also been asked to bring the matter before Parliament by many Members of this House. The case is well known to you. Count Werner Schimmelmann had his sister entrapped into the People's Hospital under the pretext that she was insane.

'It is true the Countess has led a life very different from that of most ladies of her rank. I will not dwell upon this, but merely call your attention to a little book she has just brought out under the title of "A Home Abroad," and "Among Berlin Socialists."

'I will only speak of the motives with which the incarceration was made, and the excuses used to account for it.

'These were, that she had a pistol, and was possessed by an insane fear of persecution. Both these charges are untrue.

I admit that she possessed a pistol for twenty-two years. She always had it whilst she was a Lady of Honour at the German Court, and nobody ever suspected her on that account of being insane. Moreover, when Mr. Pontoppidan met her, she had no pistol at all—it was lying at that time packed away in a bag.

'It is not true that she believed herself to be persecuted by her family. I spoke to her for a long time only a few days before her incarceration, and, though she talked a good deal about her family, she never mentioned that they were persecuting her, but only regretted there should be an estrangement between them.

'She was subject to the rudest and most disgraceful treatment whilst in the People's Hospital, and the newspaper reports of the matter are quite true. . . . A few days later I called on Mr. Pontoppidan, and requested him to let me speak to the Countess in his presence, but he refused. . . . Mr. Pontoppidan gave me his solemn promise that the Countess should not be removed until I came again, but he broke his word. When I returned I found the Countess had been taken to Ohringe. Mr. Pontoppidan, after shuffling a good deal, pretended that her dangerous state had necessitated her removal. . . . The Countess was thus brought to Ohringe, the principal Government Asylum, but was dismissed from it with a certificate that she was not in the least ill. The newspaper reports (with the exception of the *Socialdemokrat*,[1] which has indulged in a slanderous attack) have one and all spoken in favour of the Countess.

'The suggestion has been made that the Countess may have been insane when brought to the Hospital, but that she recovered on the journey to Ohringe. I deny this absolutely, and will prove it to be impossible. For, two hours after the Countess had started for Ohringe, Mr. Pontoppidan

[1] The *Socialdemokrat* withdrew the charge, and published, later on, my evangelistic address to the Socialist workmen in a most sympathetic manner.—A.S.

declared that she was perfectly insane—in fact, worse than before. But the certificate of the Head Doctor Helweg at Ohringe states that she was perfectly sane. Thus her recovery must have taken place on the journey from Copenhagen to Ohringe, a period of six hours, which is impossible.

'. . . It has been asserted that Mr. Pontoppidan, owing to his long intercourse with lunatics, may perhaps not be quite sane himself. I will not vouch for this, though there are many who believe it. It has also been suggested that Mr. Pontoppidan is a bad character, who can be bribed to get rid of people who stand in the way of their family. . . . It is certain that Mr. Pontoppidan has a bad reputation in Denmark, and there is ample reason that a thorough and impartial inquiry should be made by the legal authorities. . . .

'I have two questions to propose :—

'(1) Will the most honoured Minister of Justice bring in a bill to prevent a family with the help of a doctor putting one of their number into an asylum without the sanction of the authorities ?

'(2) Will the most honoured Minister of Justice have a thorough inquiry made into the conduct of matters in the Sixth Ward of the People's Hospital, especially as to the treatment of the Countess Schimmelmann while there, as well as to the fact of her having been brought there at all ?

'Is it not both illegal and indefensible ?'

PRESS NOTICES

Avisen—Thursday, October 17, 1894

'A Christian Martyr in Denmark in the year 1894

'. . . Here in Europe we no longer murder Christian evangelists, but we crucify them still, only by other means. What has Countess Schimmelmann not endured as a punishment for not only preaching, but also living a Christian life ! . . .'

Aftenbladet—Friday, October 12, 1894

'A modern Eleanore Christine (daughter of the king, married to Uhlfeldt, and imprisoned though innocent).

'Countess Adeline Schimmelmann's history reminds one in a striking degree of that of the unhappy daughter of the king. Both belong by birth to the highest circles of our land. Both are condemned to imprisonment—the one in a miserable prison, the other in the horrible cell of a lunatic asylum. Both suffer for their loving hearts. The one sacrifices all for her husband, the other gives all she has to the neglected and oppressed. Both are highly gifted, deep religious characters, who at last find solace in writing a description of sufferings they have undergone.'

Copenhagen—Saturday, October 13, 1894

'The lady whose thrilling experiences have been the great topic of interest during the course of the past week, has declared that she will not rest until she has brought about a reform in the law under which persons are confined in lunatic asylums. The Countess Schimmelmann possessed a too deeply religious nature, and spent her life in relieving wants of the poor and needy. She turned her back upon the Palace and the Court in order to devote herself to visiting the cottages of the poor and ministering to their needs. In consequence of her devotion she became, in the hands of a "too genial man," the victim of an idiotic and brutal system. She is, however, doing her greatest work with the help of the Press, public opinion, and the legislature, and she hopes to bring it to a successful issue by amending the whole question of the lunacy laws, and the treatment of our sane and insane, in accordance with humanity and modern civilisation.'

Dragens Nyheder—Saturday, October 13, 1894

'It is a fact that the Countess was brought by force and treachery to the Hospital, and against her will, and nobody had any right to treat her as a patient there, whether he were the doctor or any one else.

'This aspect of the case has not been very clearly expressed by the *Berlinsk*. Thus the official declaration (of Pontoppidan) is incorrect, as it tries to prove that the Countess's forcible removal to the Hospital was justified by her mental condition—a wilful perversion of truth. . . . There is one view of the matter, to which no newspaper appears to have given sufficient prominence, and that is the rough, and indeed brutal, treatment to which the Countess was subjected in Professor Pontoppidan's Sixth Ward, which has now been brought to light. The treatment was so revolting that the mere thought of it ought to make the least educated or refined blush with shame for his country.

'The treatment there would have been enough to drive the Countess mad, however sane she might have been previously.'

Nationaltidende—July 18, 1895

'Thus she was confined in this ward by Mr. Pontoppidan amidst raving and violent lunatics, living in constant dread lest her cell, the door of which was always kept wide open, should be invaded by them. And the fact of her being in the full possession of her mental faculties must have considerably added to the anxiety she had to suffer.

'And all this took place without the necessary permission of the Government, lasting from February 21 to March 28.

'On March 28 she was sent without the order of the Minister of Justice to Ohringe. Thence she was dismissed with a certificate from the Head Doctor Helweg

O

that she was "perfectly sane," that is to say, that the certificate given by Mr. Pontoppidan was false, and that there had been no justification for her detention. . . . She was confined among raving lunatics and abandoned women, and treated in the same manner. The sudden and unmerited fall from the position of a favourite and much-trusted Maid of Honour to the Empress to that of a patient in a lunatic asylum, who is less than a human being and on a par with animals, reads like a story from the *Arabian Nights.* It was left, however, to Mr. Pontoppidan to make a true story out of this unlikely plot ; and had he been allowed to have his way, she, though perfectly sane, would have spent the rest of her life in captivity. Happily for her, she was gifted with an unusually strong will, which, together with her inherent piety, enabled her successfully to overcome the terrible situation in which she was placed. The country has a right to demand that the legal authorities shall make a searching inquiry into the disgraceful circumstances of the case.'

www.ingramcontent.com/pod-product-compliance
Lightning Source LLC
Chambersburg PA
CBHW030819270326
41928CB00007B/804